INTRODUCTION

The late Erma Bombeck said that all she knew about animal behavior she learned in Loehmann's dressing room. All I know about *Yiddish* I learned from Leo Rosten, Uriel Weinreich, Fred Kogos, Rabbi Benjamin Blech, Arnold Fine, Jackie Mason, Jerry Stiller, Larry King, Pakn Treger, the magazine of the National *Yiddish* Book Center, and my mother, Jeanette Gottlieb.

When I had a huge zit on my *"punim"* two days before my high school prom, I was told *"Es vet zich oys-hallen biz der chasseneh."* James A. Matisoff, Professor of Linguistics at the University of California, Berkeley, says, *"Dos vet zikh farheylin biz der khasene!"* ("that will heal before your marriage!")

When I asked mom the meaning of "VD," she replied, "*Vo den?* VOLUME DISCOUNT!"

Yiddish Trivia provides us with fascinating facts:

- Sen. Joseph Lieberman has had an ice cream flavor named for him: "Marshmallow *Mensch.*"

- Dunkin' Donuts urged customers to try its new bagels through the use of billboards reading, "It's worth the *schlep.*"

- Rabbi Shmuley Boteach said, "*No chuppah, no shtuppa.*"

- The title of a book by Christopher Buckley is "<u>Washington *Schlepped* Here: Walking in the Nation's Capital</u>."

- Judge Judy Sheindlin said [of her TV show], "The pay is good. I get someone to *patshke* with my face so I look good."

- "*Shayna Maven*, Inc." is a company which sells weekend casual clothes.

- The 92nd Street Y in Manhattan offered a course titled, "*Kvetching and Kvelling*: Fairy Tales of Humor and Romance."

- A "*kishen kvetsher*" is a cushion squeezer — a suitor who comes and spends the time sitting at home. A "lounge" lizard!

SO WUDDAH YA WAIT'N FOR!!
READ THE "*BUKH!*"

According to Dr. Gerhard Falk, "Before 1939, when the mass murder of the Eastern European Jews began, there were 11 million people in Europe who spoke *Mama Loshen*, i.e., the language of their mothers. *Yiddish*."

Abraham Goldfaden is known as the "Father of the *Yiddish* Theater."

Jack S. Berger considers the three "giants" of *Yiddish* literature Mendele Mokher Sforim, Sholom Aleichem and Yitzhak Leibusz Peretz. He thinks of Peretz as the "Shakespeare of *Yiddish* Literature."

Mordechai Tsanin edited the first *Yiddish* daily newspaper in Israel.

The <u>Forward</u> was launched as a *Yiddish*-language daily on April 22, 1897.

In The Second Barnhart Dictionary of New English (c. 1980), there are nine (9) *Yiddishisms*: flanken, instance, (a loan translation), boychik, zetz (both n. and v.), heimish, nudzh, tchotchke, and tsouris. In <u>Merriam Webster's 11th Collegiate</u>, the editors have included 98 *Yiddish* entries. They include: bagel, bialy, boychick, futz, goy, halvah, hoo-ha, latke, lox, megillah, meshuggener, mishmash, nudnik, Reb, schnozzle, shiksa, tchotchke, tush, Yid, and zaftig.

A Google scan of the Internet (Jan. 2004) comes up with 821,000 entries on the word "*Yiddish*" and 243,000 entries for the words "*Yiddish Language*."

John Crittenden said that one must know the following 10 *Yiddish* words to understand the chatter in Miami Beach delicatessens:

1.	Bialy	6.	Kuegel
2.	Challah	7.	Latkes
3.	Borscht	8.	Lox
4.	Gelt	9.	Maven
5.	Knish	10.	Zaftig

In 1883 the Russian government banned *Yiddish* performances, and *Yiddish* actors and dramatists joined the mass emigration westwards across Europe to Paris, London, and New York.

There's a renaissance of interest in *Yiddish* and it is being taught in over 50 universities.

Yiddish has been offered at the University of Toronto for over 30 years. Al and Malka Green endowed the University with a $600,000 gift that will help fund the school's *Yiddish Studies* program in perpetuity.

The Jupiter Crab Company on Singer Island, Florida, advertised (1999) their Sunday Brunch, which included snow crab legs and a raw bar, as follows:
"All this $19.95? That's *bupkes* for this feast."

Twenty-Fourth Street Books, LLC, published (in 2003) Dr. Seuss's "Cat in the Hat" in *Yiddish*. Translated by Sholem Berger, it is titled, "*Di Kats der Payats.*"

Mickey Katz, a "borscht jester," composed an inspired parody of the American classic, "Home on the Range" in 1947. It was titled, "*Haim Afen Range.*"

In a review of the show, "Beau Jest," Frank C. Siraguso wrote, Finally, Sarah must confront the whole mess. When will she tell Chris that she's fallen for Bob, or is it really David? And what about Bob? He's begun carrying quite a torch for Sarah, but that puts her right back where she started — another *"goyfriend"* she can't introduce to her parents.

There's a kosher Chinese restaurant in Brooklyn named "Shang *Chai.*"

Marty McCullen came up with an unwise thing to say in a given situation:
To Saint Peter:
"Oh, c'mon, the only bad thing I ever did was rob some *schmuck* to pay Paul."
(The Style Invitational)
Week 516, <u>The Washington Post</u>

Robert Salant, who was 38 years old and Jewish, was hired to take a picture of a *Yiddish* language class at Columbia. He asked the students how to say "smile" and was told *"Shmeykhel."* When the students lined up, Salant screamed, "OK, say *"schmuckel!"* — using a diminutive for the word.

Studies have shown that how a person pronounces the name of a car is an indicator of their socio-economic status. For example, a person who owns a Geo Metro or Kia normally pronounces Yom Kippur, *"Yahm Kipp'er,"* while the owner of a Cadillac normally pronounces the holiday, *"Yohm KeePoor."* While the driver of the Mercedez Benz says, "Merry Christmas."

In the 1930s, Monday nights at 9:30, WLTH would air "Songs of Israel," which was sponsored by Horowitz Margareten Matzos. Listeners were encouraged to write in to receive their free bilingual *Yiddish*/English Songs of Israel songbook.

Joe Lieberman's Jewishness fascinated reporters on the 2000 campaign trail. The Associated Press distributed a small *Yiddish* glossary to help readers understand terms like *"mensch"* and *"neshama,"* and the difference between *"tuchis"* and *"tachlis."*

The National Jewish Democratic Council (NJDC) sold buttons showing a smiling Al Gore and a frowning George W. Bush. The captions under the pics? "Gore" and *"Gornisht."*

Episode number 118 of <u>The Dick Van Dyke Show</u> was titled, *"Bupkis."*

According to jewishmag.com, two popular Jewish movies are "*Balaboosta* Burn" — John Wayne's wife memorizes Grossinger cookbook, and "The Creature From The Black *Latke*" — an overdone potato pancake turns into a monster.

———◆———

Irving Kruger remade the popular standard song, "Wouldn't It Be *Loverly*" into *Yiddish* "camp":
All I vant is ah man somevere
E should dense like Fred Ahstaire
Good teeth and lots of hair
Oy, vouldn't it be loverly . . .

———◆———

The New York Times reported that a Manhattan woman walked up to the receptionist's desk at a gynecologist's office and announced: "I need to schedule my next Pap *schmear*."

———◆———

A "*schmear* campaign," according to Lenore Skenazy, is a political ploy wherein candidate fondly invokes any and all Jewish relatives no matter how distant.

———◆———

Robert I. Bernstein defined the term, "*Oyez Oyez*" as follows: *Yid.* Mutterings of a judge upon seeing Alan Dershowitz in the courtroom.
New York Magazine Competition

———◆———

In the National Review Magazine, a review of Walter K. Olson's book, The Rule of Lawyers, was titled, "*Shyster* Heaven."

———◆———

Molly Picon, the petite, effervescent star of vaudeville, Broadway and the *Yiddish* theater, taught Kate Smith and Carol Channing to sing in *Yiddish*.

———◆———

Jennifer Medina wrote, "It is a quirk of two calendars. While St. Patrick's Day always falls on March 17, the date of Purim follows the Jewish lunar calendar. So tonight, for the first time in 19 years, the Irish, the Jews and anyone eager for mischievious revelry with a little drink can get together, as Purim begins at sundown." On March 17, 2003, The New York Times carried the following headline:
IT'S BLARNEY MEETS *CHUTZPAH*,
OVER RED WINE AND GREEN BEER.

Both *"shtick"* and *"kibitz"* are included in the spell-check function dictionary of Wordperfect.

"Luftmensch," according to the 2004 <u>Page A Day Calendar</u>, is a quirky word.

The first reported use of the word *"chutzpah"* (in a state judicial opinion) was in Williams v. State (1972), an opinion of the Georgia court of appeals addressing an individual who broke into a sheriff's office to steal guns. The decision in Williams was written by Judge Clark who went on to write opinions using the *Yiddish* words *"schmooze," "tsoriss," "shammes,"* and *"gut gezacht."* The word *"chutzpah"* was used in decisions by district courts in Iowa, Alabama, and Puerto Rico.

"Shiksa lust" reached its fullest expression in <u>The Heartbreak Kid</u> (1972). Charles Grodin leaves his Jewish bride (Jeannie Berlin) to pursue the golden girl of his dreams, Cybil Shepherd.

PHILOLOGOS (Forward: Arts & Letters) says that "Among New York Jews, in any case, the *Yiddish* word *"shpritz,"* literally a 'splash' or a 'squirt,' often referred to as plain seltzer. (The word *"seltzer"* itself comes from the German Selterser Wasser, named for the town of Selters in Germany, whose springs had a naturally bubbly water.)

The cover blurb to the cooking video, "No *Shmaltz!"* is as follows: "*Tsuris* in the kitchen? Same old shpil for your meal? Cook like a real bube or zeyde, but without all the *shmaltz*. Learn to make *heymish*, low-fat delicacies with the one and only cooking videotape in *Yiddish!* NO *SHMALTZ!* is a 30-minute collection to easy-to-prepare international Jewish recipes, redesigned for a healthy heart and a slim waistline . . . Traditional *Yiddish* shtik, *Yiddish* songs and Jewish music add a lively Yidishe tam to your culinary endeavors. *Yiddish* student? Whet your appetite for learning *mame-loshn!* Don't know *Yiddish?* Just follow the subtitles: cooking is even more fun *af Yiddish."*

Yiddish misunderstandings abounded in a legislative debate a few years ago that still make lawmakers wince. On the floor of the legislature, Rep. Robert Reichert referred three times to a "poor *smuck*," with tickets to a football game. He says he thought it meant a poor soul.

Then Mitchell Kaye, a representative who <u>is</u> Jewish, tried to explain to House Speaker, Tom Murphy, that Mr. Reichert probably meant to, say *schlemeil* (a fool), or *shlimazel* (an unlucky person). But the explanation just angered Mr. Murphy, who tends to view Mr. Kaye as a *kibitzer*, or giver of unwanted advice. Mr. Murphy called Mr. Kaye a "*smook*," which rhymes with juke and doesn't mean anything. "I don't know any *Yiddish*," says Mr. Murphy.

───────────◆───────────

Alan Cagan of Lawrence, New York wrote, "I must repeat what every Jewish father asks for every year [on Father's Day]. "*nachus from der kinder*," which means pleasure from the children. Beats the hell out of a crappy tie. And my *kinder* just presented me with a granddaughter. Now that's *nachus*!"

───────────◆───────────

Alan Levy said, "During my dialogues with [famous Jewish Nazi-hunter Simon] Wiesenthal, I wondered what the Hebrew interpreter Luis de Torres, who was the first member of the expedition to set foot in the New World, might have said to the 'Indians' when the Pinta, Nina, and Santa Maria landed in the Bahamas on 12 October 1492: 'Did he address them in Hebrew?' 'That I don't know,' Simon said, adding deadpan, 'But I can tell you what the Indians said back to the white man!: 'Now begins the *tsuris*' [*Yiddish* for "troubles"]."

───────────◆───────────

"<u>Just-*tzedekah*.org</u>," is a Web resource for donors to Jewish charities.

───────────◆───────────

There's a famous <u>National Lampoon</u> "Teach Yourself *Yiddish*" piece that recommends you make up vaguely German/Russian-sounding words that start with "sch" and just string them together. One example could be "schlattwhapper" (shlat' wap ur) — A Rich Hall & Friends <u>Sniglet</u> meaning n. The window shade that allows itself to be pulled down, hesitates for a second, then snaps up in your face (*punim*).

Eli Zabar, owner of Eli's Bread, E.A.T., and other restaurants in New York City, wrote, "Today, they call it attention-deficit disorder, but my mother's word for it was the *Yiddish* "*shpilkes*."

Henry Youngman wrote a scathing op-ed piece for <u>The New York Times</u>. It was called *"Nem Di Gelt"* — Take the Money.

Renta *Yenta* was a party-planning outfit originally based on Long Island, New York

---

In Sex and the City, Harry Goldenblatt (Evan Handler) said to Charlotte York (Kristen Davis), "I never thought a *shiksa* goddess like you would fall for a *putz* like me." (Handler, 42, married a shiksa goddess of his own, Elisa Atti, in October 2003.)

In 1994 a New Jersey girl, Giordana Shabot, married Richard Shalom. What a *bashert* match — Shabot-Shalom!

<u>Zipple.com</u> listed the following Jewish movies on its web site:

"The Cincinnati *Yid*" — Steve McQueen uses some of his poker winnings to start a reform congregation.

"Singing in the *Ch'rain*" — Gene Kelly gets horseradish on his umbrella.

"*Furnished*," according to Robert B. Brown, is a fanciful definition: *Yiddish* , pert. to one too poor to afford a warm winter coat.

Robert M. Hertzberg, Speaker of the Assembly, published a 36-page brochure titled, "*Yiddish* for Assemblymembers." He said, "I want to make sure members don't get *farblondjet* when us *alter kakhers* of the Assembly make a *megillah* about our bills."

In 1903, the Jewish Daily Forward reported that a new word had entered the *Yiddish* language: "*oysesn*," or "eating out." To dine out — not at a friend's or relative's house, but at an actual restaurant — had been unheard of in the old country (and up until that point, even in the new). The Forward noted that this stylish habit was "spreading every day, especially in New York."

In Miami, Florida, big blimps fly over the beaches advertising the three K's: *kreplach*, *knishes*, and *knaydlach*.

Public School 111 in Long Island City, New York, celebrated *Oy Vey Day*. This day was devoted to an introduction to Jewish heritage. Students were permitted to complain about homework only if they slap their foreheads and yell, *"Oy Vey!"*

In 2003 a video for Jewish babies was titled, "*OyBaby*." Their press release said, "Mr. Rogers would *kvell* if he could see and hear *OyBaby*." (I should mention that Mr. Rogers would also need to be alive for that to happen.)

The theme of the eighth World Conference of the International Association of *Yiddish* Clubs, held in Baltimore from Sept. 4-7, 2003, was "*Yiddish* Teachers: Heroes Then and Now."

Saul Kahan defined the term *"schlockjaw"* as follows: speech defect endemic among politicians or talk-show hosts/guests. Early symptoms: loss of taste.

New York Magazine Competition

GoDaven.com is a Web site which lists 180 places in Manhattan where Jews can find an afternoon or evening *minyan*.

The University of Judaism offered an Elderhostel course (in 2001) titled, "*Mink Shmink*: The Influence Of *Yiddish* On America."

Linda Reck wrote a poem titled, "Ode to the *Yiddish* Language."
It said — in part:
Yiddish, it's such a
Flurry of commotion.
Ongepotchket, full of *schmutz*
And *tchotchkes*.
Hurry, dust, hurry, hurry!
Cook the *cholent*.
Bake the *babkah*, the *kugel*.
Sizzling potato *latke* sounds
Pepper the house
In preparation for Shabbat,
A day of quiet
Prayer.

(www.jewishmag.com)

———————◆———————

Time Inc. editor-in-chief, Norman Pearlstine, has dissuaded his writers from using the age-old *Yiddish* language that has given us such indispensables as *tchotchke*, *shtick*, and *schmuck*. Pearlstine says there is no official prohibition against *Yiddish* but admits he frowns on its usage: "It's not about *Yiddish* per se: I feel the same way about Latin. I have a strong preference for using English in English-language publications. I don't particularly like voilá or d'accord, or *meshugge* instead of crazy." Pearlstine also insists that if a writer absolutely has to use *Yiddish*, he or she must understand it, explaining, "If you call someone a *putz*, you should know it doesn't just mean a stupid person."

New York Magazine, 2/1/99

———————◆———————

Chai Riders Motorcycle Club is a New York Not for Profit Corporation. Chai Riders are *"Leben a guten tog"*, (having a ball); their motto: "We live to ride, but ride to eat."

———————◆———————

Detroit's Jewish motorcycle gang is called "Members of the Tribe."

———————◆———————

Toronto has its own club, "*Yidden* on Wheels Motorcycle Touring Club." YOW's logo is a motorcycle riding through the curve of the Hebrew letters for *chai*.

"*Ayzkrem*" is the *Yiddish* word for ice cream. And, according to several Web sites, Ben & Jerry's new Israeli ice cream flavors include:

Oy Ge-malt
Simchas T'Oreo
Chuppapaya
Mazel Toffee
Wailing Walnut
Bernard Malamint
. . . and all flavors come in a *Cohen*.

Rabbi Yosef Langer's motorcycle is infamous. The Chabad spiritual leader rides around San Francisco on a Mitzvah Bike. The back section is cut out to accommodate additional riders, and it is customized with a menorah and the words "Chabad of S.F. *Mitzvah Bike*" and "*Moshiach* NOW!" The *Mitzvah* Bike allows Langer to "take the message [of Judaism] to the streets."

Merriam-Webster reported that *"chutzpah"* was the hot word during August, 2000, spurred by news-coverage of VP candidate, Lieberman.

Elderhostel offered a course titled, "The Mystery and Magic of the *Bubbe Mayseh!*"

"Trayf-Busters" was an organization which rids the kitchen of any trace of *"trayf."*

Aaron Lansky founded the National *Yiddish* Book Center in Amherst, Massachusetts in 1997.

According to Marie B. Jaffe, "The Owl and the Pussy-Cat" — in *Yiddish* — reads *"Die Eyleh und Die Ketzeleh."*

A reader of The Washington Post supplied an alternate meaning for the word *"oyster"*:
    (n.) a person who sprinkles his conversation with *Yiddish* expressions.

Harry Gluckman (Harry's Humble House of Humor on the Hinternet) defines *"kinderschlep,"* as follows:
    vb. To transport other kids in your car besides yours.

Gluckman also defines *"Yidentify"* as follows:
    vb. To be able to determine ethnic origins of celebrities even though their names might be St. John, Curtis, Davis, or Taylor.

In 1991 Bill Clinton was in New York doing radio talk shows, trying to convince New York voters that in spite of his being from Arkansas, he was not an ignorant backwoodsman. One of his favorite tactics was a joke in which the talk show host asked him, "What does '*bubba*' mean?" He answered, "It's Southern for '*mensch*'."

Two *Yiddish* words heard frequently on <u>The West Wing</u> are *"shul"* and *"schmuck."*

One <u>Reader's Digest</u> Word Power quiz contained the word *"dreck."*

Rabbi Benjamin Blech calls *"drek"* The terrible "D" word. It's *Yiddish* for excrement.

The computer term "Garbage in, garbage out" (GIGO) is written in *Yiddish* as *"Drek aráyn, drek aróys."*

Shleppers Moving and Storage (1-800-84-SHLEP) is located in New York City.

A box of *Schlepper* Simon's *Yiddish* Fortune Cookies contained this message: "Smile, *Bubelah*, success is assured in 2000."

Hennie Youngman, the king of the one liners, defined a *"shadchen"* as a "dealer in livestock."

Maura B. Jacobson (<u>New York Magazine</u>, Dec. 22-29, 2003) labeled her crossword puzzle, *"Klutzy* at Christmas."

"Yid Vicious" is a Klezmer ensemble based in Madison, Wisconsin. Their debut CD is titled, *"Klez, Kez, Goy mit Fez"*; their second CD, *"Forverts!"*

In 1999 <u>Time Magazine</u> gave three examples of the "*kvetching* Jewish mother":

Sylvia Fine (Renee Taylor), <u>The Nanny</u>
Helen Seinfeld (Liz Sheridan), <u>Seinfeld</u>
Sylvia Buchman (Cynthia Harris), <u>Mad About You</u>

───────────◆───────────

Lawrence Van Gelder wrote the following theater review in <u>The New York Times</u> for Rich Orloff's comedy, "*Oy*."

. . . And with "*Oy*," in the beginning there is the word. The word is *haimish*, which the program translates as (like a family), and a new young female gentile secretary in an all-Jewish law firm is struggling to grasp its meaning and nuances, along with a lexicon of other *Yiddish* words that come flying her way.

"*Oy*" is literally hung up on *Yiddish*. Its sketches are built around *Yiddish* words like *kvell* (translated as "take pride in"), *macher* ("big shot"), *chutzpah* ("brazen nerve"), and *yenta* ("busybody"), spelled out in letters hung by the cast from a line crossing the rear of the stage.

From some of these sketches you could *kvell*. Take, for instance, "A Trolley Named *Tsuris*," which begins . . .

───────────◆───────────

Arnold Fine (<u>The Jewish Press</u>, "I Remember When") wrote a column about mothers . . . and what they would say to their children:

Abraham Lincoln's mother: "Again with the stove-pipe hat? Can't you wear a baseball cap or a *yarmulka* like the other kids?"

Albert Einstein's mother: "But it's your senior picture, *Tateleh*. Can't you do something about your hair? Maybe use some styling gel, mousse, or something!"

───────────◆───────────

Writer, Judy Gruen, discussed certain types of fears. These include receiving phone calls from the vice principal at the kids' school which begin, "Now I don't want you to worry since the bleeding finally stopped, but I thought you'd want to know that . . . The bigger and less frequent scare: receiving a fat envelope with a return address of *Gonif*, Payne & Suffern, Inc. — a law corporation."

"Nu" means Go on!, Well?, and Come on! It's one of the most frequently used *Yiddish* words.

In Rebecca Goldstein's novel, "The Mind-Body Problem," Renee Feuer achieves Phi Beta Kappa and magna cum laude status at Barnard. Her mother sighs sadly, *"Nu,* Renee, and will this help you find a husband?"

Lucille Waldman passed a listing of future services to be held at an Upper West Side (NY) church. The following subject was the title of a coming sermon:

"THE WHOLE *MEGILLAH.*"

"Der frask" is the *Yiddish* word for "the slap." In "Yentl's Revenge — The Next Wave Of Jewish Feminism," edited by Danya Ruttenberg, we learn that "There's the Jewish women's custom of slapping her daughter at the time of first menses and telling her, 'Now you know, a woman's life is hardship and pain.' "

Henry J. Stern, director of NYCivic, wrote a piece (Jan. 9, 2003) titled, "So Far, We Get *Bupkis.*" It began,

> It won't take 1776 words to tell you what the city is likely to receive from the state this year. It will take one word. *Bupkis.* The word is *Yiddish.* Its literal meaning is: goat droppings. Figuratively it means: nothing of value.

Benjamin and Jerrold Sadock wrote a piece in the Forward titled, "Finding a Niche, *Mameloshn* Goes Mainstream." They discuss the *Yiddish* word *"bubkes"*:

> In the Old World this word referred to the beanlike excremental product of goats. But use it in this sense in English and your listener won't understand *bubkes.* The tendency for a *shmutsy Yiddish* word to take on a relatively sanitized meaning in American Jewish usage is widespread. In *Yiddish,* they were strong words. In English, they're cute.

Bloomingdale's ran the following ad in 1994:

WHAT IF YOU LOVE TO SHOP, BUT HATE TO *SCHLEP*? Our Beatrice Dale consolidated shopping service is for you. Go to the Balcony; they'll give you everything you need, then shop 'til you drop. You won't carry a thing, and you only pay once.

A Dear Abby column said, "The difference between the *Yiddish* and the British is: The British leave and never say good-bye, and the *Yiddish* say good-bye and never leave."

Liz Smith wrote in 1995:

Tom Hanks was pretty emotional as he accepted his second Oscar in a row, putting him right in there with the great, Spencer Tracy, who won consecutively for 'Boys Town' and 'Captain Courageous.' But maybe Tom was so *farklempt* because he was thinking about the additional profits his win will generate.

Comedian Billy Hine reported that plans for Israel's first McDonald's advanced with an agreement that a *kibbutz* will grow potatoes to the restaurant chain's specifications. They will be called *mensch* fries.

In 1992, the 92 Street Y in Manhattan, offered Course No. BL50T01-04: "*Kvetching* and *Kvelling*: Fairy Tales of Humor and Romance" by Betty Lehr.

Description: Meet Janet Rubin and Richard Cohen — she's been planning the wedding for years, while he's been avoiding it. Meet Sima, who lived through one revolution and three husbands. Sing along with an ode to "Chicken Soup." . . .

Ben Stein said, "*Kike* is a low Polish word meaning the nastiest, most alien connotation of Jew."

According to Dvorah Telushkin, a well-known storyteller, in English, a poor man is a pauper, a beggar, a mendicant, and a panhandler. "But in *Yiddish* you can say: A poor *shlemiel*, a begging *shlimazl*, a pauper with dimples, a *shnorer* multiplied by eight, a *shleper* by the grace of God, an alms collector with a mission, a delegate from the Holy Land, dressed in seven coats of poverty, a crumb catcher, a bone picker, a plate licker, a daily observance of the Yom Kippur fast and more and more."

———————◆———————

"Kike" is a derogatory word, slang for Jew.

———————◆———————

Marlon Brando used the word *"kike"* on Larry King Live:

"Hollywood is run by Jews; it is owned by Jews — and they should have a greater sensitivity about the issue of people who are suffering. Because . . . we have seen . . . the greaseball, we've seen the Chink, we've seen the slit-eyed dangerous Jap, we have seen the wily Filipino, we've seen everything, but we never saw the *kike*. Because they knew perfectly well, that this is where you draw the [line]."

———————◆———————

The Tivoli Terrace in Westbury, New York, offered a dinner/theater show titled, "The Godfather's Meshugener Wedding."

———————◆———————

Arthur Polgon wrote to Enid Nemy at The New York Times (Metropolitan Diary):

Dear Diary:

I was helping out a tenant who operates a kosher take-home food store and had to pick up a hot pan of chicken. I had only one rag towel and asked an employee, who is Mexican, to please hand me another. He looked at me and I repeated my request, but I could see he didn't understand.

Just then the manager came up and said: "Ask him for a *shmatte*. He doesn't know what rag towel means." (*Shmatte* is rag in *Yiddish*.)

I asked the manager why he didn't teach him English words. The employee, who overheard the exchange said, "I thought *shmatte* was English."

Ellen Shulman Baker, a Jewish NASA astronaut, told her mother, Claire Shulman, once Queens (NY) Borough President, that she was studying *Yiddish*. "I learned *eppl*," she said. "What's that in English?" her mother asked. "Apple," the kid said.

American Jewish families first became acquainted with Maxwell House in the early 1920s when its parent company, Cheek-Neal-Coffee advertised in the *Yiddish* press. "It's a *mitzvah* to tell you that this Passover you won't have to turn down the pleasure of your favorite drink," proclaimed one such ad, drawing unabashedly on the language of the seder service. "No longer will you have to make do with a glass of tea at the end of the seder. You can have a cup of coffee instead, for Maxwell House is now *Kosher* for Passover."

Sheldon Landwehr, who writes restaurant reviews in the New York Post and elsewhere, rates restaurants as follows:

> What the *** mean
> 0 - *Farkackt!* (Beneath contempt)
> 1 - Unremarkable, but acceptable
> 2 - Good
> 3 - Very good
> 4 - Outstanding

There's a half-hour video titled, "*Shvitz*: My Yiddisheh Workout." With English subtitles, it also teaches how to say push-up and shoulder-shrug in *Yiddish*, while providing musical accompaniment ranging from klezmer to 1940's opera. It's a bona fide *fraylech* workout.

According to Martin Marcus ("The Power of *Yiddish* Thinking,"© 1971),

Tweed is GOYISH	Shantung is YIDDISH
Miniskirts are GOYISH	Cleavage is YIDDISH
Gout is GOYISH	Ulcers are YIDDISH

According to Leo Koppel, a non-derogatory word for non-Jew, is "*nit-yid.*"

According to Calvin Trillin (<u>The New Yorker</u>), "one *Yiddish* word that all New Yorkers are familiar with is '*kvetch*' — which actually means "to complain.' You often hear them say to each other, 'quit *kvetching!* — to no apparent effect."

In 1991, Rabbi Joel Y. Zion gave a lecture titled, "Humor and Irony in the Bible and Talmud: Where Did Woody Allen and Jackie Mason Learn Their *Schtick?*"

Jackie Mason said, "The word '*oy*' by itself cannot be considered hateful. If you're hit by a truck, you might say '*oy.*' Any time a Jew is in shock he says '*oy.*' "

A wisecrack defines a *shadchen* as "a marriage broker who knows the perfect girl for you — and married the wrong girl himself."

Brill's Content (December 1998/January 1999) reported that there was a 250 percentage increase in sales for the book <u>OY VEY!, The Things They Say!: A Book of Jewish Wit</u>, in the two weeks following the release of independent counsel Kenneth Starr's report, which mentioned that Monica Lewinsky gave the book to President Clinton.

A lucky tie is "a *malzdiker shnips*" or in more East European style, "a *mazldiker kravat.*" Sen. Lieberman wears his lucky tie — a 1970 mauve tie with cream polka dots — to every election.

The 2003 <u>Oxford Dictionary of English</u> contains the following new *Yiddish* terms:

Bashert	*Pareve*
Bubbie	*Schlimazel*
Bubkis	*Tochus*
Ganef	*Tsuris*
Macher	*Zayde*

"A *Besere Velt*," (A Better World) is a 75-member Massachusetts multigenerational chorus which performs *Yiddish* folk music.

The Country Yossi Family Magazine has a section titled, "Can't You Just *Plotz*."

In 1994, Robin Gorman Newman wrote a book titled, "How to meet a *mensch* in New York: A Decent, Responsible Person Even Your Mother Would Love."

According to Michael D. Fein (Yiddishkeit, *GantsehMegillah.com*), *"kishkeh"* is stuffed derma. It's also used to describe a person's innards. "You sweat your *kishkehs* out to give your children a good education, and what thanks do you get?"

The Little Prince was translated by Shlomo Lerman into *Yiddish* and is called *"Der Kleyner Prints."*

Hal Cantor, author of the comedy, "The Bonus Round," wrote a master's thesis for New York University titled, "*Shtick* Happens."

Seymour Kleinman, a corporate lawyer, feels that laughing is the secret of Jewish survival. In 1983 he said that he was born in SBN — South Bronx "*nishdugedacht.*"

The *Yiddish* word for mathematics is "*Mathematik.*" Arnold Fine ("I Remember When!") wrote a story in 2001 about the *yenta* who told the storekeeper that "7 and 7 is 11!" Her explanation:

> As far as I know, 7 and 7 is 11. Let me explain. You see, I already had 4 children when my first husband died. When I married a second time, my second husband also had 4 children from his first wife. After getting married, we had 3 children together. So each of us actually had 7 children, and together we had 11! You see how simple it is. Obviously, 7 and 7 is 11!

A *"gontzer k'nocker"* is a man who does <u>The New York Times</u> crossword puzzle in ink.

———————◆———————

"Farshemt" is the *Yiddish* word for ashamed.

"Farshemen" means to embarrass, to disgrace.

"Farshem nit dein mamen" means 'Don't shame your mother'.

———————◆———————

Rabbi Jon-Jay Tilson retold the following story by the late Philip "Chick" Chasen:

> During the War when I was in England, my friend was invited to go to the home of a prominent family in Leicester for the Passover seder. But he couldn't go, so I went instead. Each member of the host family was highly educated, and each one read from a Hagada in a different language. The young boy in the family spoke French, flawlessly. I read along in Hebrew.
>
> After the seder, the father of the family said, "Phil, where did you learn to do that? You read so fluently and proficiently that when I paused to take a breath, you kept going. Where did you learn to do that?"
>
> And all I could think of was *"Farshem nit dein mamen."*

———————◆———————

There's a business in Manhattan named "Candle *Shtick.*"

———————◆———————

Miriam Weinstein (<u>*"Yiddish — A Nation Of Words"*</u>) explained how you can tell when a woman is ready to deliver. When she calls out in French, mon dieu, you send for the doctor. When she cries in Russian for her mama, *memushka*, you know her time is approaching. But when she screams in *Yiddish*, 'dear God, *gottenyu'*, you know she is ready to deliver.

———————◆———————

An Israeli company developed a perfume which they hoped would compete with Chanel No. 5. It was named *"Chutzpah."*

"Abi Gezunt" (As Long as You're Healthy) opened on Oct. 3, 1949, at the Second Avenue Theater in New York City. It had originally been 40 minutes too long and Yonkel (Molly Picon's, husband, began to cut. He was called a regular *mohel* (freely translated, Yankee Clipper).

"Beryiah," according to Bubba's Yiddish Glossary, is a *baleboosteh* squared; a regular Martha Stewart. A homemaker who puts the rest of us to shame.

Albert Vorspan ("My Rabbi Doesn't Make House Calls A Guide to Games Jews Play") discussed how to build a temple: The Jewish Edifice Complex. The caterer can advertise: "Visit Our Unique Drive-In Synagogue, Where the Posh Come to *Nosh*."

Judy Gammon invented a name based on an inherited business: *"Chaim Glatta Meetcha* — Scion of the Tel Aviv Welcome Wagon founder, Israel Plezure."

(New York Magazine, Comp. #815)

Joan Ruttenberg suggested that *"Yentl Ben"* — a young bear disguises itself as a boy in order to study the Torah — be a summer replacement TV pilot.

(New York Magazine, Comp. #943)

"Friends in *Chai* Places" is a Long Island (NY) organization.

"Quirks, Idiosyncrasies and *Mushugass"* is the title of an book by Judy Reiser.

Hiram Brown (who adapted the popular "gumps" comic strip to radio drama and in 1929 he worked with Gertrude Berg to create "The Rise of the Goldbergs"), never got into *Yiddish* radio. WEVD approached him but he said, "I decided I just couldn't hear 'Inner Sanctum' in *Yiddish*." (He patented the sound of the 'Inner Sanctum' creaking door.)

The March 18, 2003 issue of <u>The Palm Beach Post</u> carried the following obituary:

DUDL (DAVID) BERNSTEIN

Died Tuesday, March 11, 2003, while giving his best conducting the *Yiddish* Folk chorus of Palm Beach County at a concert in Miami Beach.

All his life he was involved in both the *Yiddish* language and *Yiddish* folk music. The members of the chorus will miss him greatly for his leadership, his musical ability, his friendship, and his strong feelings for the *Yiddish* language.

He believes that a *"Folk Vos Zingt Vet Kainmol Nit Unter Gain"* — A people that sings will never die.

Members of the *Yiddish* Folk Chorus
of Palm Beach County Florida

When Colin Powell took to the stage at the American Israel Public Affairs Committee Conference in Washington (2001), he made it clear that he believed he was among friends. He had been rumored to be fluent in *Yiddish*. "Well, yes, I do understand a *bissel*, (i.e., "a little"), he said to laughter.

A (1956) New York law case, Zannone v. Polino, involved *kibitzing* at a card game, which ultimately turned into a knife fight.

Isaac Galena. (Bangitout.com), "Dividing things into . . . 'Jewish' and '*Goyish*' wrote,

E-greetings and palm pilots are *goyish* forms of communication. Instant Messenger is the Jewish way to *schmooze*.

The entire idea of '<u>Designing Women</u>' was *goyish*. '<u>Golden Girls</u>' screamed Jewish.

"*Schmooze* Your Way to the Top" is a chapter in Dan Zevin's 1994 book, "<u>Entry-Level Life — a Complete Guide To Masquerading As A Member Of The Real World</u>."

asked the following question on their "Who Knows *Yiddish"* Quiz:

> Q. 3: I'm in *Yiddish* math class. This is the problem I'm stuck on: *'zekhtalk'* plus *'finf'* plus *'dray'*, plus *'tsvey'* equals _____.
> (Answer in *Yiddish*)
> The correct answer is *"zibetsik."*

Nuyenta.com is a Jewish matchmaking service.

Andrea Carla Michaels, a Jewish puzzle constructor and Scrabble teacher says, "The hardest part of course is the different spellings of the (*Yiddish*) words . . . there are like seven different ways to spell *ganef/goniff*. *YENTA* can also be *YENTE*. (Why? Go know!)" Fred Kogos spells it *"yenteh."*

In 2002 Michael Freund wrote a piece on "Jewish Heritage Day" at Shea Stadium. It was titled, "Seventh-inning *Kvetch.*" In between innings, an Israeli dance troupe played the tune "Hava Nagila."

"The *Oy* of Flex" was the name of an article by Mark Adams in the March 1997 issue of GQ Magazine.

The Actors Temple (Cong. Ezrath Israel) in Manhattan, has a free community Hebrew school on Sundays — "The Little Red *Shul* House."

Michael Steinberg ("Still Pitching — A Memoir") wrote, "At thirteen. I was called a *'shlepper'* — a slightly awkward but not entirely inept athlete."

At the Academy of Jewish Studies in Florida, they offered an Elderhostel course titled, "Dress British, Think *Yiddish:* Assimilation Is A Two-Way Street!"

Peter Hochstein ("Up From Seltzer — A Handy Guide To 4 Jewish Generations"), defines English-*Yiddish* Grammar:

> Another way to give special emphasis to a declaration is to advance the direct object of a verb to the head of a sentence.
>
> Ex.: "Trouble I could live without."

———◆———

The Jewish Retreat Center at Camp Isabella Freedman in Great Barrington, MA, offered the following Elderhostel course in 1997:

> "Use Your *Kop*": An Intergenerational *Yiddish Yontiv!*

———◆———

In September 2001, Americans celebrated "Love a *Mensch* Day."

———◆———

"Fun, *Frum*, and Fit" is a Sunday workout program offered by the Washington Heights and Inwood Y, a UJA-Federation beneficiary agency. Cyndi Rand, director of the Y's Jewish Culture & Education Dept. says, "Exercise changes your life. It's a *mechayeh* [total relaxation]."

———◆———

Time Magazine reported that Democrats went in on the eponymous ice-cream war and came up with these two flavors: "Marshmallow *Mensch*" — Full of tasty marshmallow chads and meets the strict kosher standards of a council of rabbis; "Key Limeberman" — the sweet fellow who wants everyone to get their fair share of the pie.

———◆———

In 1990, Daniel Siegel gave a lecture on the topic, "What Does Bruce Springsteen Know About *Mitzvot* That We Don't Know?"

———◆———

New York State has the most *Yiddish*-speaking people. When zip codes are used, the Williamsburg neighborhood has a greater number of *Yiddish* speakers than Borough Park. However, when "NYC neighborhoods," are used, Borough Park has a greater number of *Yiddish* speakers than Williamsburg.

The Web site "*Yiddishamama*," offers Jewish jokes daily. One recent example: What's the difference between Karate and judo? Karate is a form of self-defense, and judo is what bagels are made of.

"In *yam arayn*" means "into the ocean," according to Berish Goldshteyn (<u>yugntruf@yugntruf.org</u>).

In Dara Horn's book, "<u>In The Image</u>," she tells a story about Jews immigrating to America. When the ship pulled into New York Harbor, immigrants went up on deck to see the Statue of Liberty and their new home. Some of the Jewish immigrants weren't just looking out at the city. They were throwing their *tefillin* overboard, convinced that in the New World they would no longer need them.

Rabbi David P. Hochman says that the above story sounds more like a metaphor than a news report. Just like someone may 'drop their emotional baggage' or 'leave their inhibitions at the door.' There have been thriving religious Jewish communities built by immigrants in New York, Chicago, Philadelphia, and elsewhere since before the waves of immigration in the 1890s & 1920s, so I don't attribute much value on such a blanket statement. Mark Twain's 'the report of my death was an exaggeration' can be applied to many other modern novelists who may be projecting their issues with Jewish identity onto their characters.

Rabbi Berel Wein wrote about *tefillin* being thrown overboard:

> "Whether such acts actually took place is not provable, either way, now over a century later. However, the phrase throwing *teffilin* in the Hudson became the descriptive folk-saying to describe the rapid assimilation of the immigrant Jews and their giving up on Torah observance."

Isaac Bashevis Singer said, "*Yiddish* has vitamins which no other language has. We should never lose the idioms and vitamins of our mother tongue."

"Dos gefil" means "feeling sensation."

Gefilte Fish, according to Kosher.nosh, is explained as follows: "Jacques Cousteau (*alev a sholem*) is still looking for it."

Mensch Films was founded by filmmakers Mark Ostrick and Ezra Soiferman.

Margaret Cho, Korean-American comedienne, referred to herself as *"ziftig."*

The word *"zoftig"* was used in Tony Kushner's 2003 HBO production of "Angels in America." Also included in this avant-garde play was the expression, "Wasps don't say '*feh.*'"

Dunkin' Donuts urged customers to try its new bagels through the use of billboards reading, "It's worth the *schlep.*"

Rabbi Sam Silver defines a *"shiksa"* as an electric shaver for women.

Rabbi Benjamin Blech says that *"Oy,"* isn't a word — it's a vocabulary.

According to Wilhelm Maurer, *"Chuzpe"* (as it is spelled in German), "implies also topping an already bad/shameless/impudent/ behavior. One well-known definition of *chuzpe* in Austria is:'*Chuzpe* has somebody who goes into the opera house wearing just a bathing suit, and deposits it at the wardrobe.'"

Oyveyauctions.com donates 18% of all pretax profits to charity.

"Gib a kuk" (give a look) at how these <u>New York Magazine</u> readers define these *"Oy"* words:

Susan Harriman defines *"oyez"* as follows: Heb oy, expression of dismay, + Ezra, Hebrew scribe, A.D. 50. Cry of attention during a legal proceeding.

David Rozenson defines *"oyez"* as follows: from *Yiddish oy vey izmir* (colloq.: you think you have problems); hence, the call which marks the opening of a court session.

Peaches Clar defines *"oyster"* as the kvetchman, whine-meister, gripe-atollah.

Joel Sitrin defines *"oyster"* as follows: from Heb. *oy*, expression of woe, plus comb. formster. Upset over the ruinous Assyrian invasion, Hezekiah complained to god, who told him to quit his *kvetching*. Thus, an extremely taciturn person.

B. Schmulivitz defines *"oysgegrinteh"* as one who makes her husband wash the dishes and mop the floor while she goes to the movies with a boarder.

———————◆———————

Ingrid Peritz (<u>The Globe and Mail</u>) wrote the following obituary for Dora Wasserman:

Wednesday, December 17, 2003

MONTREAL — If there were murmurs of *oy vey* on the streets of Montreal yesterday, the lament was understandable: Dora Wasserman, *maven* of Montreal theatre and champion of the *Yiddish* language, had passed away.

Ms. Wasserman's raw willpower helped keep alive a language whose death notice had been signed more than once. She believed *Yiddish* was all about survival, and it drove her to stage plays in the Displaced Persons camps of Europe, and later to found the only resident *Yiddish* theatre in North America.

Danielle Kichler gives an alternative definition for *"kvetch"*: someone who, when asked, "How are you?" tells you, usually at great length and in full detail.

Jon Siegel said that one Jewish wag (possibly the humorist Sam Levenson, well-known in the 60s and 70s) defined *Chutzpah* as "Enough gall to be divided into three parts."

In the book, "Reaper Man" by comic fantasy writer, Terry Pratchett, there is a character called "*Schleppel*," who's a bogeyman.

Nahum Stutchkoff published his *Yiddish* rhyming dictionary in 1931, and won him great renown among playwrights, intelligensia, and the general *Yiddish* public.

Nahum Stutchkoff published a 933-page *Der Oytser Fun Der Yiddisher Sprakh* (Thesaurus of the *Yiddish* language). The tome contained 392 synonyms for the word "hit," more than 100 words and expressions for "*chutzpah*," and seven pages of curses — inverted blessings, mostly, since cursing is forbidden in Judaism. One example: "You should have a hundred houses; in every house a hundred rooms; in every room twenty beds, and a delirious fever should drive you from one bed to the next."

Sid Caesar ("Caesar's Hours — My Life in Comedy, With Love and Laughter") wrote, "I'm pretty sure I'm responsible for introducing the word '*chutzpa*' into the American vernacular. I remember looking for the right word in a sketch and blurting out, 'That guy has an awful lot of *chutzpah*.' "

Dr. Richard Gorman said, "there is another connotation to *"shlep"*; to have influence, e.g. 'He got his kid into the programme because he has *shlep* with the Board.' "

Amy Menell calls the religious skullcap for women, a "*Yamaha*."

In 1987, E. D. Hirsch, Jr. wrote a book titled, "Cultural Literacy: What Every American Needs To Know." Included in the list of nearly 5,000 terms was the word "yarmulke."

———◆———

When Sid Caesar played Shtaka Yamagura, a samurai warrior, he and his brothers interspersed Yiddish words like shmo, which sounded Japanese, into the dialogue. They also used a lot of Yiddish words for character names because they were just funny: Baron Kasha and Gantza Metzia.

———◆———

According to Harry Leichter's Jewish Humor, "Chutzpah," is going to the psychiatrist because of a split personality, and asking for a group rate.

———◆———

Debbie Tuma, a Daily News reporter, wrote in 1998, "Seinfeld made a star out of Jason Alexander. Its done bubkes for Mike Costanza — the guy on whom the George character is based."

———◆———

Fred Kogos ("A Dictionary of Yiddish Slang & Idioms") defines "Gifilteh fish" as stuffed fish (usually made of chopped fish, onions and seasoning, and cooked in salt water). The New York Aquarium used to have a commercial in which they said, ". . . we have all kinds of fish — except Gefilte fish."

———◆———

The label on "Soy Vay" — Veri Veri Teriyaki, reads:

"Our company came to be when a Jewish boy and a Chinese girl began talking about a common interest: cooking. We soon realized that by combining the best of our families, cooking secrets, we could create new and unique tastes. The result — Soy Vay!" K Parve.

———◆———

"Plotz," according to Martin Marcus, means to explode. To fall apart as with laughter or overeating. At your mother's dinner you have two choices: to eat like a normal human being and disgrace her, or to eat as she tells you and PLOTZ.

"Overdressed Prez must have been a Boy Scout" was the title of an article written by Linda Stasi of the New York Post. She discusses how President Bush wore more gear than Inspector Gadget, when he flew on the USS Abraham Lincoln during May of 2003. "How Dubya would ever have stayed afloat with all that *oisgepotzed* hanging off him had he been forced to bail out, no one can say," said Stasi.

The *Yiddish* word *"plotz"* means to bust, burst, or explode. *"Plotz"* was also a Parker Brothers game which came out in 1971.

"Plotz" was defined by Nancy Gibson Nash as "to sicken after reading too many screen plays."

"SNOW FALLING ON SEDERS — Memories of a Minnesota *Mohel"* was the title for an "Authorized Autobiography" supplied by Albert W. Katz for New York Magazine's Competition #961.

According to Henry Sapoznik, Producer of The Yiddish Radio Project and winner of the 2003 Peabody Award, Mandy Patinkin did not know any *Yiddish* before performing in the show, *"Mamaloshen."* Sapoznik and Michael Wex translated the vast majority of the songs he used on the CD. Sapoznik coached him in pronunciation and performance of the songs.

Frumster is an Orthodox Dating Service for sincere singles in a serious search for their soul mates. Since its launch in December of 2001, at least 156 members have found their soul mates through this service. Their number of confirmed matches is at 78, but they are sure there are more. This number represents couples who have actively come forward to let *Frumster* know of their success.

Mandy Patinkin (*"Mamaloshen"*) said, "But I began singing the song 'Youssel, Youssel' and I found it had a hook like a fishing hook that grabbed your *kishkes* (innards) and threw you all over the room like a big pike being pulled out of the ocean."

The *Yiddish* word *"frum"* means pious or devout.

———————◆———————

Larry King ("When You're From Brooklyn, Everything Else Is Tokyo") wrote about his childhood meal times: "To leave something on the plate was not only wasteful but insulting to the cook and bad for your health." Others say that Jews had so little, there were no leftovers. Leftover food is *"ibergelost essen,"* or *"iberblayb"* or *"shirayim."*

———————◆———————

Patricia Sommers wrote in the Washington Post (2/11/99) about Mandy Patinkin in *"Mamaloshen":*

> And for those left wanting more at the conclusion of the piece, Patinkin, wizardly pianist Paul Ford and virtuosic violinist Saeka Matsuyama end with a casual but no less brilliant string of the singer's English-language specialties. Highlights of Tuesday's performance included the wonderfully frenetic "Beat Out That Rhythm on a Drum" (Oscar Hammerstein's gloss on Bizet's "Carmen"), a charming commingling of Stephen Sondheim's "Everybody Says Don't" and Frank Loesser's "The Emperor's New Clothes," and a dreamy English-*Yiddish* finale of "Over the Rainbow" that left the huge crowd *kvelling* — the *Yiddish* word for rhapsodizing.

———————◆———————

A reviewer for New York Magazine said of "Mamaloshen":

> "The mere sound of his voice would make Moses *'ferklempt.'* "

———————◆———————

"Usavegelt.com" is a consumer oriented website/organization. Their motto: "Prices Hard to Beat; Service Hard to Meet."

———————◆———————

Stephen Mark Dobbs, a Jewish Bulletin correspondent said, "There is something momentarily riveting about the President of the United States or a super movie star telling a colleague to 'stop *kibitzing.'* "

"*Lipshtick* Creative Concepts" is a comedy firm that develops exercises and live theater around corporate issues.

According to Jackie Mason and Raoul Felder's book, "Survival Guide to New York City" (1997), these *Yiddish* words are considered necessary for survival:

Ahf Tsu Loches	*Kishkes*
Billik	*Oy Vey*
Chozzer	*Schlemiel* or *Schlimazel*
Chutzpah	*Schlock*
Feh	*Schmear*
Fumfer	*Schmuck*
Goy	*Shmatte*
Handle	

There's an ironic expression in *Yiddish* that translates: "That's a *Kulikov* trial." It comes from something that allegedly happened in a small town in Poland (or maybe Russia, or Lithuania, or Hotzenplotz) called, yes, *Kulikov*. This town was so small, it had only two tailors and one shoemaker. The shoemaker went crazy (maybe because he was the only shoemaker) and killed someone. So they held a trial, and the shoemaker was found guilty and sentenced to hang. But we're talking about the town's only shoemaker here, so they hanged one of the tailors instead.

According to Milton Berle, "A *brisket* is a Rabbi's toolbox."

Michael Wolff, New York Magazine (Sept. 7, 1998) writes about Steven Brill (Brill's Content):

> "The stories of his financial ups and downs, his deals, his battles, his *chutzpa*, are legion . . . He is what my father used to call 'an operator.' "

Joe Grossman (Time Out New York, July 31-Aug. 7, 2003) wrote, "*Oy*, Canada, Montreal's Just for Laughs Festival, offered as much to *kvetch* about as it did to *kvell* about." ("Just for Laughs" is the world's largest comedy festival and the biggest laugh.)

The following headlines appeared in the second issue of Heeb
Magazine:
"Word To Your *Bubbe*"
"Urban *Kvetch*"
"*Bubbe*-Licious"
"*Schvitzshop* Shutdown"

◆

"*Shlock* rock" is a parody CD with titles like "Bring Back that
Shabbos Feeling" and "*Woodshlock.*"

◆

According to *haruth.com/YSyiddishinLaw*, the earliest reported
case that uses a *Yiddish* word (other than in a name or a literal
quote) is in re Kladneve's Estate (N.Y. 1929) which describes Kladneve
as "what is called in *Yiddish* a *schmorer.*" There is no such *Yiddish*
word, and *"schnorrer"* — the closest word that might fit — means
"moocher." This isn't a very nice thing to say about the recently
departed.

◆

Judith Shulevitz, a regular contributor to The New York Times
and Slate, wrote the following about the TV show, "The Goldbergs":

". . . Molly's warmhearted intrusiveness seemed about as
appetizing as a *schmear* of *schmaltz* on Wonderbread."

◆

Irene Backalenick wrote a (2002) review of *"Schmaltz"* in the
Forward:
New off-Broadway show at the 78th Street Theatre Lab is
appropriately called *"Schmaltz!"* In fact, it glorifies the
cholesterol-raising, blood-pressure threatening Jewish food of
old. Gefilte fish with horseradish, chicken fat on pumpernickel,
and all the rest get a proper tribute, as well as instructions
for preparation. But *"Schmaltz,"* offered by the husband and
wife team of Mark Zeller and Dana Zeller Alexis, is a good
deal more than a food show. It is in fact a sharp profile of
one Jewish family.

Zeller's comedy . . . is about Benny, who Is going through a
mid-life crisis and longs to find elusive happiness in the
comforting foods he knew as a child: challah bread, Gefillte
fish, egg creams and chicken fat sandwiches.

According to Richard F. Shepard ("How Yiddish *Shlepped* to Conquer"), ". . . *chutzpah* elbowed its way into American English with the unmitigated gall of an introder. It may have reached its zenith when, in writing about Nikita Khrushchev's banging his shoe at a meeting of the United Nations General Assembly, James Reston introduced it in his column on the August editorial page of The New York Times to describe his misbehavior. *Chutzpah*? At the United Nations? So what else is new? *Nu*?"

———◆———

In the book, "How'm I Doing? The Wit and Wisdom of Ed Koch, Mayor of New York City — An unauthorized edition" by Mel Shestack and Sayre Ross, three Koch *Yiddish*-isms are included:

(1) "They're making a big *tsimmes* out of it."
(2) "Stop with your *megillah*."
(3) "You don't agree? Well, *gezinterheidt*."

———◆———

Ed Koch's favorite words (most used in quotes) are:

Vile	Richies
Outrageous	Unforgiveable
Betrayed	*Schmuck*

———◆———

August 25, 2000

An article about a visit by Vice President Al Gore and Senator Joseph I. Lieberman to a Jewish community center in Florida misattributed a *Yiddish* greeting. It was Lieberman, not Mr. Gore, who said, *"Shalom aleichem"*; Mr. Gore said, *"Mazel tov."*

———◆———

Larry Wilde ("The Last Official Jewish Joke Book — maybe next to the last") contained this *Yiddish* joke:

Did you know that Manischewitz just bought out the Christian Wine Co.?

They're going to change the name to *Manischaygetz*.

———◆———

A Little Bit Klezmer, Y'All? "Tennessee *Schmaltz*" is a klezmer band whose music is a combination of Jewish, Appalachian, and jazz.

Kosherman.com offers Jewish Fortune Cookies with different delightful sayings.

Ex. YOU WILL MEET A REAL *MENCH* — TALL, DARK, AND CALLS HIS MOTHER EVERY DAY!

———————◆———————

"Manilow, The Sultan of *Schmaltz*," was the name of a <u>New York Times</u> article on April 6, 2002. "Manilow," refers to singer Barry Manilow (Barry Alan Pincus); "*schmaltz*" refers to high-cholesterol styles of music and tear-jerking drama.

———————◆———————

Libby Mowshowitz ("<u>Straight Talk From A Rabbi's Wife</u>") says that "Grandparents have more '*nachas*' than parents. They have '*nachas*' from the children, '*naches*' from their grandchildren, and '*nachas*' when their children have '*nachas*.' "

———————◆———————

"*Fancy-shmancy*" was a term that appeared in the vaudeville sketches of Potash and Perlmutter, Smith and Dale, and others.
This "*fancy schmancy*" joke has been circulating on the Internet:

Able and Sadie had worked for years in the shmata business. Finally, they made it big, very big, and to get a little legitimacy they gave a big gift to the local orchestra. As a thank you for their contribution, they are invited to a very *fancy schmancy* dinner party. At the party, Sadie looks around for an entree to this most impressive crowd. Hearing a group of ladies discussing Beethoven, she senses her chance; "Beethoven?" She says, "happens I know him very well. In fact, just the udder day I saw him on the number five bus going to the beach." There is a hushed silence. Everyone is embarrassed by Sadie's faux pas. Abie feels utterly humiliated. Back in the car, on the way home, Abie says to Sadie, "Vat's the matter vit you? You couldn't sit qviet like a duchess? You had to open your big mouth? Everybody knows the number five bus doesn't go to the beach!

———————◆———————

The <u>New York Press</u> called Peter Cooper Village a plush, *fancy-schmantzy* oasis. It has its own park, its own recreational facilities, underground parking — even free concerts for the residents.

Marjorie Ingall wrote a column in <u>The Forward</u> mocking the whole 92nd Street Y *mishegas*:

> As you may remember, a financial analyst asked a Citibank hotshot to help get his twins into the coveted *fancy-schmancy* preschool, which features a retractable playground roof and the opportunity to have graham crackers with the offspring of self-important fantric-sex-practicing elderly rock god Sting. Back then, the notion of getting your kid into the "right preschool" seemed amusing and loony to me. These days I'm a bit less sanguine.

Lenny Bruce, a well-known Jewish comedian from the 1960s, explained the meaning of *"goyish"*:

> If you live in New York or any other city, you are Jewish. It doesn't matter even if you're Catholic; if you live In New York, you're Jewish. If you live in Butte, Montana, you're going to be *goyish* even if you're Jewish.
>
> Kool-Aid is *goyish*. Evaporated milk is *goyish* even if the Jews invented it. Chocolate is Jewish and fudge is *goyish*. Fruit salad is Jewish. Lime Jello is *goyish*. Lime soda is very *goyish*.
>
> All Drake's cakes are *goyish*. Pumpernickel is Jewish and, as you know, white bread is very *goyish*. Instant potatoes, *goyish*. Black cherry soda's very Jewish, macaroons are very Jewish.

"Farblondjet" is the title of a 2003 play by Jeremy Kareken at the Epic Rep Theater in New York City. The Website describes the play as the story of a young man who "looks for love amongst the ruins of a dying civilization — the Catskills, There he finds the one love he can't have, the father he never liked, and a whole lot of *tsuris*."

A Jewish gay group in Montreal, Canada, is called *"Feygelah."*

The character *"Shmendrick"* was introduced in <u>The Two KuniLemis</u> (Fools), and the name has entered the contemporary American lexicon as a synonym for bumbler, nincompoop, or fool.

In 2003, Carol Newman formed *"The Oy Project"* — *Oy* — One Yelp — might help! She suggested that this Rosh Hashana every Jew around the world, give a unified sign, a groan, a cry — an *OY!!!* to show that we have had enough, indeed too much.

OY! — enough terrorism.
OY! — enough bloodshed.
OY! — enough loss.
OY! — enough hatred.
Oyyyyyyyy!!!!!!!!

There's a Klezmer Band named "*Yiddishe Cup.*"

The abbreviation "VD" means "venereal disease." In *Yiddish*, "*Voo Den?*" (What else?), and "volume discount."

Sukkot.com advertises a *"Klutz-proof"* sukkah kit.

The word *"tseshmetter"* means to smash into pieces. To clobber. "What happened to the Mets today?" They were *"TSESHMETTERED".*

Source: "*Yiddish* for Yankees, or Funny, You Don't Look Gentile" by Martin Marcus.

"*Di menopoyze*" is the *Yiddish* word for menopause, according to Dr. Mordkhe Schaechter ("Pregnancy, Childbirth and Early Childhood, An English-*Yiddish* Dictionary").

Rabbi Debra Orenstein said that "Jewish tradition has been silent for a lot of years about *menopause* and other biological passages that women go through, and the losses and stresses that these passages represent." And Laura Pulfer (The Cincinnati Enquirer) wrote,

Hundreds of Websites are devoted to "The Change." Everything from "Menopause Made Easy" to something called the "Gifts of Menopause." As if we didn't know what these "gifts" might be. Facial hair. Mood swings. Hot flashes. Weight gains. Memory loss. (Please, Mother Nature, I beg of you. Take me off your gift list.)

The *Yiddish* words for error are *"der grayz"* and *"der toes."* <u>The New York Times</u> — and other newspapers — make errors. Linda Amster and Dylan Loeb ("Kill Duck Before Serving — Red Faces at <u>The New York Times</u> — A Collection of the newspaper's most interesting, embarrassing and offbeat corrections") included these:

> September 20, 1998
> . . . It was "<u>Fiddler on the Roof</u>," not from *"Der yiddisher H.M.S. Pinafore."*

———————◆———————

<u>The New York Times</u>, Education Life, Section 4A/August 3, 20031 contained the following headline:

> "College guidebooks have become as fat as the phone book. Let your fingers do the *schlepping.*"

———————◆———————

Dan Pine, writer for <u>The Jewish Bulletin of Northern California,</u> wrote a piece about *"Yiddish* for Scrabble? Wordsmith in S.F. Spells it out." (<u>URL: http://www.jewishsf.com</u>)

K-R-E-P-L-A-C-H
5-1-1-3-1-1-3-4

You place the "P" on a double-letter square, the word on a triple word score. That's 66 points for the word, 50 points for the bingo (using all seven of your tiles), totaling 116 points. Yes!

Red-faced and irate, your opponent immediately barks: *"Kreplach?* That's not a word! Certainly not a word in the Scrabble dictionary. I challenge."

Smiling, you casually flip through the Scrabble dictionary to page 311. You clear your throat: "Ahem . . . '*Kreplach:* dumplings filled with meat or cheese.' "

———————◆———————

In the movie, "<u>It Runs in the Family</u>," Kirk Douglas (86) piles into a fishing boat with his son, Michael, and grandson, Cameron. *"Shmuck!"* Kirk calls Michael at one point in the film. (Michael told film critic, Joel Siegel, that it was his father's one ad-lib in the movie and that Kirk's been waiting years to call him that on screen.)

———————◆———————

"Truskavke" or *"trushkaveh"* means strawberry in *Yiddish.*

Three guys are about to be executed, and they are asked what they wish to have for their last meal. The Italian responds, "Pepperoni Pizza," which he is served and then he is quickly executed. The Frenchman requests a Filet Mignon, which he is served and then he is promptly executed. The Jew, using his *Yiddishe Kop*, requests a plate of strawberries.

STRAWBERRIES??

Yes, strawberries.

He is told, "But they are out of season!"

"So, *nu*, I'll wait!"

GOYESHA KUP

A Jewish *yingl* finds a *gut shiksa* to marry.

She decides to convert and be taught everything Jewish and Hebrew by *der rov.*

Finally, a date is made for her to go to the *mikva.*

The day before she goes to *der sheynkayt-salon* (beauty parlor) to have her hair done and now dresses up for the *mikva* ceremony.

Der rov at the *mikva* tells her to enter *dos vaser.*

"Now dunk your head."

But, she answers, that she just had her hair done and can't dunk her head.

So *der rov* replies: "If you don't, you will remain a *goyesheh kup kop!*"

A *"maven,"* according to Robert Hendrickson ("New Yawk Tawk"), is a *Yiddish* term, pronounced, *MAY-vin,* for an expert on something; from the Hebrew for "understanding." One can be everything from a pickle *maven* to a Beethoven *maven.* Also spelled *"mavin."*

Rosie Einhorn and Sherry Zimmerman ("aish.com") explain the duties of a mentor:

"Mentors may have to serve as handholders for singles who have developed a wonderful relationship with someone who is right for them, but need positive reinforcement and encouragement to help them decide to become engaged . . . get through the normal anxieties and stress of engagement . . . distinguish between pre-marriage jitters and genuine problems with a potential spouse . . . and even survive a few bouts of cold feet and make it to the *chuppah.*"

A Mike Myers character on <u>Saturday Night Live</u>, Linda Richman, used various authentically *Yiddish* expressions such as *"farklempt"* and *"shpilkes."*

In the play, *"Tzipke,"* Molly Picon's husband, Yankel, had a line that got a big laugh: "My father is a *'shikker'* (drunk)." Molly answered, "A *groiser shikker"* (big drunk).

Calvin Trillon said, "The remarkable thing about my mother is that for thirty years she served us nothing but leftovers. The original meal has never been found."

"Iberblaybns" is the official *Yiddish* word for leftovers. The word *"shirayim"* is probably more colloquial.

Professor Raphael (Refoyl) Finkel has compiled an extensive list of computer terms in *Yiddish*, they include, for example:

click (of the mouse: noun)	*klik/kliks, shlisl, knakl*
error	*der toes*
execute (cause program to run)	*baarbetn, derfirn*
formatting	*tsure*
hot key	*heys-klavish*

For a complete list, check out this URL:
http://www.cs.uky.edu/~raphael/privatel/terminology.txt

The <u>Zagat Survey</u>, 1999/2000 New York City Market rated Ess-A-Bagel (831 Third Avenue, New York City), as follows:

The "best bagel in NYC" proclaim the myriad fans of the "bodacious," 'life preserver-sized beauties turned out by this duo, which just edges out H&H in the quality category; the bagels are "soft," "chewy" and always "fresh", because "long lines" mean they "never stick around long enough to cool down" — just brace for "chaos on weekends" and note that servers may throw in a free *"schmear* of attitude."

Ron Kurtus (www.school-for-champions.com) published a piece titled, "Was Gerald Ford Really a *Klutz*?"

Shmuel is on his deathbed, and he knows it. Hardly able to breathe, he tells his wife: "Ruchel, call the priest. Tell him I want to convert." His wife is thunderstruck. "All your life, you were a *frumer yid* (pious Jew) and now you don't want me to call Gutterman's Funeral Home. Have you lost your senses?" Chaim looks at her and weakly whispers, "Isn't it better a *goy* should die than a Jew?"

＊

Rabbi Perry Netter is the author of a book titled, "Divorce is a Mitzvah."

＊

Martin Bodek's quiz (Bang-itout.com) titled, "Who Wants to Marry a Boro Park Millionaire?" asked the following $2,000 question:

How do you say the word "cucumber" in *Yiddish*?

A) *Kartofel*   C) *Igerkeh*
B) *Tzibileh*   D) *Gebeks*

The correct answer is (C).

＊

"*Oi-Va-Voi*" are a six-piece band featuring the guitar, drums, bass, clarinet and violin. "*Oi-Va-Voi*" is a *Yiddish* colloquialism that stands for "Oh my God!" It fits the Klezmer tradition of not taking things too seriously.

＊

Pete Hamill wrote [in part) in the introduction to the paperback picture book, "NYC: Life Goes On" (which went on sale Sept. 11, 2003),

"Nobody in New York looks afraid. Too busy working, arguing, struggling, *kvetching*, lying, sometimes brawling, sometimes weeping. Too busy making art and dance and song. Too busy loving. Too busy living."

＊

In the late 1950s, a common Israeli joke told of a mother on a bus berating her child in *Yiddish*, giving him a *"klap"* whenever he replied in Hebrew. When a stranger asked why she beat the child who spoke such good Hebrew, the mother answered, "I want him to know *Yiddish;* he shouldn't forget he's a Jew."

An article by Brian Montopoli in the Sept. 2003 issue of the Washington Monthly was titled, "*Schlep* to Judgement — If anything merited an independent inquiry, it was the attack on 9/11. But not in Bush's Washington!"

———◆———

An article on backpacking gear, by Eileen Daspin and Robert J. Hughes in the Weekend Journal of the Wall Street Journal (Sept. 19, 2003) was titled, "Walking *Shtick*."

———◆———

A ($1.75) Designer Greetings Inc. card had the following printed message:

"A *Yiddish* Anniversary wish for a *glickloch* pair . . . Your friends and your *mishpucha* are all agreed on this: You're a pair of loving *menchen* and you share the greatest bliss! So may life be a *mechaieh*, and may love grow *shtarker* yet for a *Yiddish* Romeo and a Jewish Juliet! Happy Anniversary."

———◆———

"*Narrishkeit*" is the *Yiddish* word for foolishness. Here is one example of Jewish humor from Cong. Beth Or (www.bethor.org/narrishkeit/narrish.html)

If you can't say something nice,
say it in *Yiddish*.

———◆———

Henry Hollander, a book dealer in San Francisco who has a substantial *Yiddish* collection, has the following Website address:

boychik@hollanderbooks.com.

———◆———

There was a scandal when the word "*schmuck*," was accepted by the crossword puzzle editor, Will Weng, apparently unaware that the word is "a person of bad character" as well as the course vulgarism for "penis." Will Shortz, present crossword puzzle editor at the Times, says, "And times do change. I would use the word SCHMUCK in a puzzle now, fully aware of its etymology. In its English meaning, the dictionaries label it slang, not 'vulgar.' "

The Web site, "jjdaily@Laughmeister.com (*Yiddishamama*) told the following joke:

> How many Jewish mothers in law does it take to change a lightbulb?
>
> None, they'll just sit in the dark. They know you can't be bothered to do a simple thing like change a lightbulb for them, and after all they've done for you.

In The Odd Couple, cast member Joanne Sanchez, the daughter of Anne Berger, said, "We had so much fun [during the shoot]. We were kidding around. I'd call him [Walter Matthau] up and say, 'This is Senorita Sanchez.' He'd call me 'Seniorita,' or '*Tchotchkeleh*.'"

Yiddish words have appeared in defamation cases. A 1972 New York case concluded that calling the food at a restaurant "ground-up *schmutz*" wasn't actionable because it was only opinion.

At the annual (2002) Jewish Heritage event held at Assembly Hall at Hunter College, New York, Gov. George E. Pataki and former Mayor Edward I. Koch performed a skit in *Yiddish*. Actor Tony Randall, delivered Hamlet's "To Be or Not to Be" soliloquy in *Yiddish*.

Michael Lewittes of the New York Post (February 7, 2001), wrote a piece titled, The Hardest Job is the Job Interview. His opening paragraph begins,

> "LIKE *yentas* in the winter, the economy is also heading south, which is why so many people are now out of work."

In the 1920s, Molly Picon starred as a *Yiddish*-speaking Peter Pan for some 3,000 performances.

In 1954 Molly Picon toured Israel, playing benefit performances in *Yiddish*. While there, she spoke before the Knesset on the importance of preserving the *Yiddish* language, even among Hebrew-speaking people.

Molly Picon's country home in Mahopec, New York, was called "Chez *Schmendrick.*"

Walter Matthau (born Walter Matasschanskayasky) took on the role of intellect by portraying Albert Einstein in the 1994 film, "<u>I.Q.</u>" He talked at the time about what he might say to Einstein: "I probably would have told him some jokes in *Yiddish.* He enjoyed *Yiddish* jokes and since I knew a lot of those, we would have gotten along splendidly."

Benny Leonard (born Benjamin Leiner) spent over seven years as the world lightweight boxing champ, from 1917 to 1924. During his tenure as champion, some synagogues offered a *"gomel benshen"* — a prayer of thanksgiving — on the Sabbath following each of his successful fights.

"<u>Ketskil Honimun</u>" was a 1930s musical filled with Borscht Belt *"shtik."*

Mickey Katz's greatest *"shticks"* included:

"She'll Be Coming 'Round the Katzkills"
"It's a *Schlemiel* of Fortune"
"*Borscht* Riders in the Sky"
"Barber of *Schlemiel"*
"It's a *Michaye* in Hawaiye"
"*Poiple* Kishke Eater"
"*Yiddish* Mule Train"

One of Steve Martin's stage acts, The Great Flydini, consisted of pulling a series of outré objects — for instance, eggs — from his unzipped fly. That was his *"shtick."*

There are several variations for the *Yiddish* word for chef: *"der groissa cuisiner," "der moloch dem kishkas machers,"* and *"der ganza farbrenter fum alles."* And, according to Al Thomas, a kosher hotel named Teplitzky's in Atlantic City, had an American Indian named Frank Halfhide as the chef.

The *Yiddish* word for name is *"nomen."*

There's a classic *"nomen*-changing" joke. A fellow encounters an old classmate. He shouts, *"Shmuel* Rabinowitz! Haven't seen you for years!" *"Shah,"* he admonishes, "that's not my name anymore. Too old-fashioned, old country. Now I'm C.D. Rivingston." "How'd you think of that?" "You know I used to *shlep 'frukht'* on Rivingston Street." "Then what's the C.D.?" "Corner Delancey."

Dr. Barbara Held ("Stop Smiling, Start *Kvetching:* A 5-Step Guide to Creative Complaining"), invented the term "creative *kvetching"* — complaining that not only makes you feel better, but helps your listener empathize. Her first two steps: 1. Your Inalienable Right to *Kvetch*; 2. You Can't *Kvetch* to All of the People All of the Time.

David H. Bader ("Haikus for Jews") wrote,

Yenta. Shmeer. Gevalt.
Shlemiel, Shlimazl. Tochis.
Oy! To be fluent!

When asked about the origin of the *Yiddish* expression, *"What am I, chopped liver?"* Ask the Rabbi replied:

The phrase was coined in America. Chopped liver is a side dish and never a main course, so the phrase is used to express hurt and amazement when someone feels overlooked, i.e., treated as a "side dish."

Jimmy Durante recorded that famous line: "Now that ain't chopped liver!" Today Jews say, "What am I, chopped liver?" Lenore Skenazy (New York Daily News columnist) wrote the following lines to a song titled, *"You Gotta Be Lieb"* (To "O Tannenbaum"):

Oh Lieberman, Yeshiva-man
How beagle-sad your face is
I know that you would feel less blue
If you and Dean switched places
You gave Gore all you had to give
He treated you just like chopped liv
Oh Lieberman, dead meat-erman
Too bad that's what a race is.

"Gehakte leber iz beser vi gahakte tsores" means chopped liver is better than chopped-up troubles.

------------◆------------

Nicholas Lemann (The New Yorker, Whodunit Dept., The Anthrax Culprit), wrote,

> Barbara Hatch Rosenberg, a slight woman with short graying hair and deeply concerned hazel eyes, who works out of a small office at the State University of New York at Purchase, thinks she knows who was responsible for the attacks last October. Rosenberg is, to use the technical term, not *chopped liver . . .*

------------◆------------

The titles of the three books by Sir Arthur Conan Doyle, which were translated into *Yiddish* are as follows:

> *"Der grester detektiv an intersanter shtudyum fun oyserardentlikhe menshilikhe fehigkeyten* (A Study in Scarlet)" Translated by D. M. Hermalin.
>
> *"Fantazye un virklinkhkeyt!"* Translated by S. Zaks.
>
> *"Oysgevelte ertseylungen"* Translated by S. Zaks.
>
> > Aaron Rubinstein
> > Collection Manager, *Yiddish* Book Dept.
> > National *Yiddish* Book Center, Amherst, MA

------------◆------------

According to Richard F. Shepard and Vicki Gold Levi ("Live & Be Well — A Celebration of *Yiddish* Culture in America"), the waiters in Ratner's dairy restaurant, New York City, had a habit of telling the diner who wanted *borscht* that he really wanted *"kreplach."*

------------◆------------

Mark Blei wrote the following Jewish Haiku lines:

> Scrabble anarchy
> after *'putzhead'* is
> placed on
> a triple-word score.

------------◆------------

In a Guide to Studio *Yiddish* (www.hollywoodsapphiregroup.com), the word *"tchochkes"* means bells & whistles, doo-dads; similar to *chozzerai*, but better quality.

The *Yiddish* word for "bedbug" is *"vantz"* or *"vants."* There was an entire <u>M.A.S.H.</u> episode entirely based on Hawkeye needing to remember the *Yiddish* word for bedbug. Hawkeye had gotten a <u>New York Times</u> Sunday crossword and struggled with the *Yiddish* clue/answer. He called a friend for help and that friend flew into the M.A.S.H. unit mistakenly thinking there was some medical emergency.

There are 22 noodle-kugel-*lokshen* recipes, as well as maps of the *Yiddish* speaking areas of Europe in Rabbi Robert Sternberg's book, "*<u>Yiddish</u> <u>Cuisine: A Gourmet's Approach to Jewish Cooking.</u>*"

The *Yiddish* word for heartburn is *"harts-brenenish."* Jeannie Sakol and Jeanne Sakol wrote, "<u>Nouvelle Yenta Cooking: Farewell to Heartburn Hotel.</u>" The contents page lists the following chapters:

> La Prune De Ma *Tante*
> You Could Fool Your Grandma
> *Challah* Go Lightly
> Secrets of the *Maven*

On the "<u>*Oy!* Everything Jewish</u> Links Page," the editors write:

> *Oy!* When the rest of the world turns you down saying, *"Drai mir nit kain kop,"* we'll offer help. What are you looking for? Jewish food, Jewish jokes, Jewish schools, something about Israel, Jewish support groups, Jewish law? We have links to all. If your son wants to marry a *shikseh*, we have links to people who will advise you. We'll even help you learn *YIDDISH*, so that when your grandmother yells at you, at least you'll understand.

And this P.S. follows:

> The authors and editors of this site assume no responsibility for the information contained herein. Do not be a *shmuck*, we couldn't know everything.

"Frau *Farbissina*" (AKA "Mindy Sterling") is the frowny Austin Powers character.

One of the most memorable scenes in the landmark film, <u>Blazing Saddles</u> depicts a Sioux chief (Mel Brooks) drawing his horse up to a black family during an Indian raid on a wagon train. He says, in *Yiddish*: "*Zeit nisht meshugge. Loz em gaien . . . Abee gezint.*" (Don't be crazy. Let them go . . . As long as we are all healthy." (No translation was provided, but audiences generally understood Brooks, linking Indians, Blacks, and Jews as historic underdogs who could use a helping hand in a cruel world.

Budd Mishkin, a sports and features anchor for the NY 1 cable channel, performed "*Borscht in the USA*," an evening of Bulat Okundzhava favorites like "*Mu za tzenoy nye postoyim*" (We will pay any price) and "*Soyuz druzeiy*" (a union of friends) in Manhattan in 2003.

According to Maira Kalman and Rick Meyerowitz (<u>The New Yorker</u>, September 8, 2003), "What's New In Pharmacology," under ANTIPEPSIODINES, we find "*kishkafix*" and under PANDEMONICS, we find "*Schwarzeneggre*" (Shtarkazine).

"*Shtup*" has several meanings: a push, a shove, a sexual episode, and a fornicator.

Actor Dustin Hoffman said (in 1993), "I like everything about it but the word grandfather." (He opts instead for the name "*grandshtupper.*")

Molly Picon had the only *Yiddish* swimming pool in the world, according to Marnie Winston-Macauley ("A Little Joy, A Little *Oy*"). At three feet, the pool side sign read, "A *mecha'yeh* [a pleasure]," at five, "*Oy vay* [it's getting a little deep in here]," and at ten feet, "*Gevalt*" [HEELLPP!]

Bank Leumi once ran an ad campaign that said, "You may have a friend at Chase Manhattan, but with us you have '*mishpuhe*.' " (They also said, "If it took six days to create the world, why should it take four weeks to get a loan?")

Calvin Trillon wrote in <u>The Nation</u> (March 9, 1992): Croatians are the good guys now,

> Although their past is slightly shady.
> So worry not that these same guys
> Chased both your *bubbe* and your *zayde.*

A "*Shul* Shirt," according to Wendy Greene, is dowdy, yet dressy-enough clothing, worn to *shul.*

"*Ahftseloches*"— according to the *Yiddish* Dictionary of the Tri-City JCC in Tempe, AZ, is defined as follows:

> n. inevitable bad luck. The result of a *kinehora* promotion and you have a piece of spinach lodged between your front teeth. *Aftseloches,* you think. Something like this had to happen.

"*Kvetch,*" according to Richard P. Horowitz, is defined as follows:

> *Kvetch* - [ModYid]
> to complain obsessively about trivial or unalterable conditions, thereby showing that you are not yet brain-dead. See *mishigas.*

"*Ershter*" means first. The first ever Passover (Pesach) seder over the internet took place on April 3, 1996, and was held at Congregation Emanu-El in New York City.

Leonard Wolf's translation of <u>Winnie-the-Pooh</u> — in *Yiddish* — is "*Vin-der-Pu.*"

Jennifer Traig and Victoria Traig's book, "<u>JUDAIKITSCH,</u> <u>Tchotchkes, Schmattes and Nosherei</u>", provides instructions on how to make the "Neil *Tzedakah* Box," a "Mah-Jongg Menorah," and "the *Borscht* Belt."

Herb Geduld wrote a piece for the Cleveland <u>Jewish News.com</u> titled, "How a 7th-inning *Kvetch* became 7th-inning Stretch."

Justice Antonin Scalia utilized *"chutzpah"* in a formal Supreme Court opinion paper.

According to Robert Hendrickson ("<u>New York Tawk</u>"), the expression "make with" means to use or exercise, as in "He's making with the voice again, but he can't sing a note." Possibly from the *Yiddish* expression *machen mit*, "swing something about."

The Jewish Theological Seminary Library owns approximately 7,400 volumes of books in the *Yiddish* language.

In 1994 David "Dudu" Fisher played Jean Valjean on Broadway for the first time. On his dressing room door was his name and the part he played, and underneath was the name of the actor who replaced him on Friday nights. In brackets, someone added *"Shabbos Goy."*

July 12, 1883, marked the infamous *"Trafe* Banquet" in Cincinnati, where shrimp (decidedly a non-kosher item) was served at the party for the first graduating class of American Rabbis. Only two rabbis walked out; others simply pushed the "unclean" tidbits aside. The details of this banquet were published by a young woman, a stringer for the <u>Jewish Messenger</u>, who signed herself Sulamith. Her name was Henrietta Szold.

"Ganefs" was the title of a comic strip by Harvey Kurtzman and Bill Elder in the premiere issue of <u>MAD</u>. It was a crime story of a brilliant gangster and his bumbling cohort.

The January 1994 cover (No. 324) of <u>MAD Magazine</u> contained the following words:

"YOU CAN FOOL SOME OF THE READERS ALL OF THE TIME . . .

THESE ARE THE *SCHMUCKS* WE'RE AFTER"

— Abraham E. Neuman

"Yeshivish" is a new Yiddishism pertaining to the world of the Yeshiva, as in "He dresses too *yeshivish,*" says Kobi Weitzner.

In the new *"Joys of Yiddish"* (edited by Lawrence Bush), the word *"faygeleh,"* the *Yiddish* word for homosexual, is omitted.

An *"imerman"* or *"immer-mahn"* is an "ex-husband"; *"imervayb"* or *"immer-vibe"* is an "ex-wife."

<u>Time Magazine</u> [April 13, 1998] <u>MILESTONES</u> wrote:

DIED. BELLA ABZUG, 77, champion extraordinaire of women, labor, blacks and any other underdog society could muster; in New York City. With the slogan "This woman's place is in the House — the House of Representatives'," she won a seat in Congress in 1970 and bowled over Washington with her in-your-face manner and her raspy voice for reform. Abzug's signature hats were as wide and as colorful as her crotchety *chutzpah.*

According to Deborah Gasiorek, the Second Avenue Deli (founded in 1954), "catered to the dedicated Jewish actors, actresses, and theater goers from the dying *Yiddish* theater district, once known as *Yiddish* Broadway or *Knish* Alley."

The Website "<u>jjdaily@Laughmeister.com</u>" (*Yiddishamama*) offered the following joke:

Two Jews visit the tomb of Baron von Rothschild.

They stand nodding in silent awe till one breaks the silence.

"*Oy,* that's the way to live."

Jack E. Leonard, the abrasive comedian ("Good evening, opponents!"), once called the garrulous moderator of a TV discussion program "a *yenta* with facts."

Dr. Kenneth Libo presented a lecture titled, "From *Schlemiels* To Big Deals: American Jews in Big Business."

"*High schmooze,*" a film and TV term, represents a Hollywood event with a high proportion of "players" in attendance.

"*Zaftig:* Well Rounded Erotica" is a book by Hanne Blank.

"When I first emigrated to America," reminisced Sam the radish exporter, "I was forced to settle in the Bronx instead of Schenectady. After all, who can spell a *meshuggeneh* name like that?"

"Classic Jewish Humor in America"
by Henry D. Spalding

"How About A Big Tax On *Kvetching*" was the title of an article in The New York Times by Joyce Purnick.

There are two *Yiddish* words for "lesbian" says Binyumen ("Ben") Schaechter:

di lezberke (singular); *lezberkes* (plural)

di lezbianke (singular); *lezbiankes* (plural)

The name *"Fyvush"* (as in *Fyvush* Finkel) roughly translates as "Phillip" in *Yiddish.*

The TV program The Nanny, starring Fran Drescher as Fran Fine, was filled with all sorts of *Yiddish* vocabulary: *bar-mitzvah, bashert, bubbie, bubkes, farkakta, kvetch, meshugeneh, meschpuche, mazel tov, oy, punim, shlep, shnoz, schnozzola, shmootz, shvits, shikse, tuchas,* and *yenta.*

"The Mah Jongg *Maven*" is a Website which sells Mah Jongg merchandise.

A *"kane"* or *"conneh"* is the *Yiddish* word for an enema.

Joel Siegel ("<u>Lessons For Dylan</u>") tells about a great *Yiddish* theater joke about the actor who falls down dead, in the third act of <u>King Lear</u>:

> "Oh, my God, he's dead!" one of the actors shouts.
> From the balcony comes a cry "Gib him a *conneh!*"
> "But he's dead!" the actor shouts back.
> "It couldn't hurt!"

Sid Caesar used many *Yiddishisms* in his skits. Some of his most memorable lampoons were:

- a Japanese skit called *"Gantze Mishpoche"*
- an Italian parody *"Gatkes"*
- a French tavern called *"Der Fligel"* (chicken wing)

"*Yiddishpiel*," the *Yiddish* theater in Israel, was established with the intention of preserving the *Yiddish* language and culture, and recognizing its fundamental importance in the literary and artistic creation of our nation.

In *Yiddish*, *"Ain minute foon shtilkeit"* means one minute of silence. *"Zol zein shtil!"* means silence!

Rabbi Anchelle Perl (Mineola, New York) offered *ET-mail* (Extra Torah Mail), suggesting that during Super Bowl XXXVIII (Feb. 1, 2004), Jews turn off *"di televisye"* (the television) right in the middle of the game for just one minute to observe "One minute of Silence" in memory of lost ones. He asked that we use the moment to reflect on true meaning in life and how each of us can add in our acts of goodness and kindness to make this a better place, especially for those less fortunate and sad at this time. "It takes a special person to tune out the jackhammering raucous of society to hear the beating of a grieving heart," says Perl. "Let us today remember the mourning families in the Land of Israel. Let us remember the many families who have lost loved ones because of terrorism in the USA and all over the world."

According to Gail Lansky, *Zamler* Coordinator at the National *Yiddish* Book Center in Antherst, MA, there are *"zamlers"* across the country that will pick up *Yiddish* books and take the responsibility of getting them to Amherst. As of Feb. 2004, there were 216 *zamlers* . . . and the number is constantly growing.

———————◆———————

Rachel Levine's Website, *"CyberYenta"* lists the following *Yiddish* sightings:

CYBER YENTA'S
Yiddish Sightings
YIDDISH SIGHTING: (n.) A *Yiddish* word or expression seen or heard in non-Jewish media.
Here's the list so far: (* = very surprising)

WORD	HEARD/SEEN
"Fahrbiseneh"	Austin Powers, The Movie
"Gribinitz"	Mrs. Doubtfire, The Movie
"Putz"	Fox News Channel. Neal Caputo
"Geshrei"	Fox News Channel. William Safire
"Shul" and *"Schmuck"*	The West Wing
"Bupkis"	Chicago Hope, Murder She Wrote
*"Fahrklimpt"**	Marathon For St. Jude — 107.1 FM Country Western Station
"Shpritzer"	Fox 5 TV, Good Day New York
"Kvelling"	New York Magazine, Gotham Section
"Shvitz"	The Sopranos
"Kishkes", *"Shvitz"*	Dharma & Greg
"Schleppers"	New York Post Crossword
"Shtup"	The Whole Nine Yards, Movie
"Nosh"	ABC Cooking Show — Firefighters trying to lose weight.
"Tushy"	Oprah Show, said by Sela Ward
"Chatchke"	Wired Magazine
"Schmaltzy"	Vanity Fair Magazine
"Shiksa"	Homicide, TV Show
*"Dreck"**	Reader's Digest — Word Power (This is now a word for vocabulary tests?)
"Zoftig"	Katie Couric, The Today Show
"Oy Veh"	Jeff Corwin, Animal Planet
"Zoftig"	Margaret Cho, Korean-American, Comedienne, referring to herself.
"Hondel"	Alex Trebeck, Jeopardy, July 2001
"Chutzpah"	Judy Dench, "As Time Goes By", BBC sitcom

In *Yiddish* , the car is *"der oyto"* and a Cadillac is called a *"Kédilek"* or a *"Kédillak."*

Rabbi Benjamin Block ("The Complete Idiot's Guide to Learning *Yiddish"*) wrote,

> "Let me start by dispelling the rumor that, for years, Jews allegedly thought another word for car was *Kedillak* . . . In reality, however, most Jews had to settle for a Karele — the diminute le not only communicates that the car they drove was smaller, but considerably cheaper."

James A. Matisoff ("Blessings, Curses, Hopes, and Fears — Psycho-ostensive Expressions in *Yiddish"*) writes,

> *"Un itst fort er arúm in a Kédilek!"*
> ("And now he's driving around in a Cadillac!")

And "Sch" as a prefix to anything, suggests disapproval.

> Ex. "Cadillac *Schmaddilac*, You're suddenly too good for the Lincoln?

Yaakov Branfman ("The Hidden World — Challenge, Adventure, and Pleasure in Giving") wrote,

> In the Mattersdorf neighborhood of Jerusalem, a bag of baby's pacifiers hangs on the fence that runs along a well-traveled road. Next to the bag is a small sign saying that anyone is welcome to take a pacifier and asked to please return a new one to the bag when convenient. Lost pacifiers can be a problem, especially if the baby wakes up in the middle of the night, as so often happens., This self-service *gemach* operates on its own all day and all night.

"Mizyukl" and *"smotshik"* are *Yiddish* terms for a baby's pacifier. Ken Blady says that the best translation for pacifier is *"smutchig."* The Hebrew word *'matzess'* has also crept into the *Yiddish* language in some circles."

His P.S.: "Don't confuse *smutchig* with *shmootshig.*"

In Israel, they just say *"motzetz."* Ex. *"Gib mir de motzetz."*

Norman Rosenblood, Ph.D. has coined the word *"moolifier"* for a baby's pacifier. He made a pun on the *Yiddish* word for mouth (*mool/mohl*) and the English word (mollify). Hence, a soother = *moolifier.*

"Moyl" is another acceptable spelling for the word mouth.

"Der eydes" is the *Yiddish* word for the witness. The 1985 movie, "Witness," has jokingly been renamed "*V*itness." One movie reviewer wrote, "If you're in trouble or running from the law, the best place to hide is Amish country."

A *"trombenik"* is a bum, a loudmouth, a ne'er-do-well (slang). In Yinglish, a *"trombenik"* is a *"blufferken."*

Brian Blum (www.ThisNormalLife.com) writes,

> You know what *schmoozing* is, right? It goes by many different names, depending on the context. At a cocktail party, it's called mingling. At a business event or conference, you know it as networking. When two or more Jews get together, though, there's no other word to use than to *schmooze*. It's undoubtedly as old as the Jewish people itself and was probably a major factor in our survival these past thousands of years.
>
> Good *schmoozing* can be done anywhere.
>
> Pounding the exhibit hall floor: "Your product is amazing. It could revolutionize the industry. I totally believe in what you're doing. By the way, here's my card."
>
> Or in the lunch line: "Excuse me, but do you think the brownies or the blueberry muffins look better today? And say, aren't you Bill Gates?"

———————◆———————

Baruch Podolsky provided the following proverb:

"*Vayt fun di oygn — vayt fun hartsn.*"

This means "Far from the eyes — far from the heart."
The English equivalent is "out of sight, out of mind."

Source: "All's Well That Ends Well"
by Dr. Yosef Guri

———————◆———————

Dr. Khane-Faygl Turtletaub, a Chicago teacher of *Yiddish* and Jewish Culture, discussed the term *"shanda."* Sometimes spelled *"shande,"* it means shame. Turtletaub says that when one Jew does something bad, it shames all Jews. "This notion came into play in the cases of Winona Ryder's shoplifting conviction and Monica Lewinsky's notorious dalliance with President Clinton," says Turtletaub.

———————◆———————

At the Chicago Seven Trial, Rabbi Marc Howard Wilson heard Abbie Hoffman shout at Judge Julius Hoffman, "It's a *shondeh far die goyim.*"

According to Arthur Schwartz, the food *maven* (www.arthurschwartz.com),

> *Maven* is a *Yiddish* word that means connoisseur; in other words, a person who can discern quality. A food *maven* could therefore also be called a gourmet, but we won't be using that word here. I jokingly refer to the word "gourmet" as the "g" word. I don't like to use it because it has become so overused and abused. After all, nowadays, even convenience stores call themselves "gourmet groceries." . . . I'm a real food know-it-all.

The occasional character on the <u>Jack Benny Show</u> was Mr. *Kitzel* (Artie Auerback), who spoke with a very thick *Yiddish* accent. The character sang the catchy little song,

> "A pickle in the middle with the mustard on the top, just the way you like it and they're all red hot."

These three episodes appeared on the <u>Jack Benny Show</u>:

5/25/32	Introducing Philander *Kvetch*
11/20/32	Jack and Sid *Schlepper*
12/01/32	*Schlepper* Visits The Office

Islan Stavens wrote a piece for the <u>Forward</u> titled, "In a Jewish-Hispanic Fairy Tale, A Witch With a *Yiddish* Accent." In his review of the movie, "<u>Sami and I</u>," he wrote,

> The plot is familiar enough: Meet Samuel Goldstein. About to turn 40, he acts and thinks like Jerry Seinfeld, Woody Allen and Mel Brooks combined into a Nathan's frankfurter. He also works in television, but — what else is new? — he hates his job. Is there a Jewish neurotic who is happy with what he has? . . . Is Samy a *schlemazel*? Or is he a *schlemiel*? His girlfriend is a Lacanian psychobabbler, his sister is depressed, and his Jewish mother is . . . well, una madre judia.

"Eh!" and *"Feh!"* were common expressions in <u>MAD Magazine</u>.

A <u>School Library Journal</u> said,

> "Though only two syllables long, *zaftig* has a certain voluptuousness about it, much like a dollop of chocolate. Derived from *Yiddish*, it means 'juicy.' "

———◆———

The following question appeared in a "Test Your *Yiddishkeit*" quiz from a 1998 <u>Jews for Jesus Newsletter:</u>

B.   Is Megillah
1. The first name of a 1960's cartoon character (last name Gorilla);

or

2. The Hebrew word for "scroll" referring to the Book of Esther, also used colloquially to indicate "the whole story."

———◆———

"New York is not for *Klutz's*" was the name of an article written by Rachel Sokol for the <u>Greenwich Village Gazette</u>.

———◆———

The Learning Annex in New York City offered a $19.95 course in their Dec. 2003 catalog titled, "Instant *Yiddish* — Talk Like a *Mensch*." The ad read:

> Do you wish you could say classic *Yiddish* proverbs like: *A falshe matbeye farlirt men nit:* A bad penny always turns up. *Nit keyn entfer iz oykh an entfer:* No answer is also an answer. *Az se brent, iz a fayer:* Where there's smoke, there's fire . . .

———◆———

"*Shlimazl*," according to Marty Fiebert, is a chronically unlucky person; a born loser. When a "*shlimazl*" sells umbrellas, the sun comes out.

———◆———

The following three terms are frequently used by Jewish and non-Jewish historians to describe the Jewish Catskills:
"*derma* road"
"*borscht* belt"
"Jewish alps"

Al Dubin was the lyricist for *"My Yiddisha Butterfly"* (M. Witmark & Sons, publisher):

"Flutter, flutter, flutter
'round your Abie Perlmutter
Oi, my *Yiddisha* Butterfly!
Ask your Fadder and your Mudder
If they want a clothing cutter
In the fam'ly by and by"

———————◆———————

A George Harrison lyric from 1989 was titled, *"Cockamamie* Business":

Well you do what you can —
can't do much more than that
(No you can't do what he just said)
Some days you're pretty sharp —
on other days you feel half dead
(While you make your daily bread).
Didn't want to be a star —
wanted just to play guitar
In this *cockamamie* business.

———————◆———————

The word *"shidekh"* is defined as a marriage match in "The Yiddish Dictionary: Sourcebook" by Herman Galvin and Stan Tamarkin.

———————◆———————

Adina Kalish produced a 5-minute video titled, "Century Village Shiddach" — a quick, cute look at how grandparents living in Florida meddle in the affairs of their grandchildren.

———————◆———————

Henryk Szaro produced a 90-minute video (*Yiddish* with English subtitles) titled, "The Vow." It's a *Yiddish* fantasy about Chaim and Mendl, two Yeshiva students who vow that if they have children of opposite sexes, the two children will be paired in a *shidduch* marriage. Their vow is forgotten until years later when the prophet Elijah gets involved.

———————◆———————

"Where There's Smoke, There's Salmon: The Book of Jewish Proverbs" was written by Michael Levin.

"Philologos," who writes a column on *Yiddish* in the English-language Forward, traces the word *Bubbe*, to two roots: Grandmother *bubbie* comes from the Polish and the Slavic "grandmother," but bubbele, as in sweetheart or good little boy, comes from the German *Bub*, or *Bube*, which goes "back to Middle High German Buobe, meaning a young man, squire, or knave, and deriving from Old High German *Buoba*, which was a man's name . . . which has been proposed by etymologists as the source of our English word 'boy.' "

Andy Abrahams Wilson produced a 35-minute, 16 mm film titled, "*Bubbeh* Lee and Me." The English film is an intimate and hilarious portrait of an extraordinary and ordinary Jewish grandmother and a touching account of her gay grandson's search for his place in the world. It was an Emmy Award nominee.

David Glick wrote a piece titled, "The Vanishing (or Vanished?) Mama" for Jewishmag.com:

The *Yiddisha Mama*, how precious she was. Songs of praise were sung to her. Men would sit and reminisce about their own personal *Yiddisha Mama*. A part of history, perhaps long ago, but still remembered by many and longed for by even more.

The *Yiddisha Mama*, a character out of the bygone era. The far away times of recent immigrants and scraping by. A personification of the truly devoted. The ever watchful eye, always concerned for her precious children. *Est, a bisle, mien kinder* — and stuff a mouth with a morsel of food.

The common ground that the long gone *Yiddisha Mama* and our Hi-tech Jewish mama share is the desire and ability to give to their children. The *Yiddisha Mama* in her time gave with her concern for her children through her cooking and sewing. Making sure that they came first and that they would get the best, much better than what their parents had.

Today's Hi-tech Jewish Mama, is concerned too, but her concern doesn't come out as chicken soup and another piece of bread stuffed in her child's mouth. Her concern comes as a desire to give to her children the best in the sphere to which she lives. Passing on the Jewish values and the concern for others. But her giving and the kindness is there, just like she received from her own *Yiddisha Mama*, waiting for the next generation to take from her and to pass on to their children.

Rabbi Simcha Feuerman and Chaya Feuerman wrote an Article in <u>The Jewish Press</u> titled, "A '*Shanda* On A Honda': When The Rabbi's Children Misbehave." They asked, "What can the Rebbetzin do if her daughter was seen on a motorcycle with a boy (hence the title of this article)?

An ad for course number 249H at the Learning Annex in New York City read — in part:

Instant *Yiddish*
With the Staff of The Workmen's Circle

Do you wish you could say classic *Yiddish* Proverbs like: *A falshe matbeye farlirt men nit:* A bad penny always turns up. *Nit keyn entfer iz oykh an entfer:* No answer is also an answer. *Az se brent, iz a fayer:* Where there's smoke, there's fire.

"Some swing and *shtick*" was the title of an article by Russell Scott Smith on the Jewish Museum's new Goodkind Media Center. Visitors can enjoy the classic comedy bits like Mel Brooks' "How to Be a Jewish Son," plus Manischewitz wine ads from the '60s with Sammy Davis, Jr. and Peter Lawford.

A *mezuzah* consecrates the home. In order to be certain mezuzot are 100% Kosher, *Halacha* requires they be inspected at least every 3 1/2 years for defects and flaws. The *Mezuzah* Doctor has inspected and sold over 40,000 Mezuzot and *Tefillin* worldwide.

Jackie Mason was appealing to the highest authority to insure that his 2003 musical review, "<u>Laughing Room Only</u>" would be "*matsliakhdik*" (successful). Before the first preview, Mason, his friend Raoul Lionel Felder, and Garment Center Synagogue Rabbi Norman Lipstokin were backstage at the Brooks Atkinson Theater affixing a mezuzah to each dressing room door. The rabbi led each occupant in a ceremonial prayer. The benediction appeared to have worked. The show's first performance got a standing ovation.

The "Chopped Liver River Band" ("*gehakte leber*") is based in Lancaster, Pennsylvania.

Three days before Yom Kippur, 2003, the Jewish members of the Friars Club met to roast the Smothers Brothers. Dick Capri approved of the choice — calling them the "Sunshine *Goys*."

Miriam Weinstein ("*Yiddish — A Nation of Words*") tells a joke long popular with American Jews. An immigrant with a heavy *Yiddish* accent and an ill-fitting name of *Shane Ferguson* was asked how he acquired such an uncharacteristic moniker. He replied that, on the boat coming over, he had practiced saying his new American name. But when on his arrival he was confronted with a frightening English-speaking cop, he could only blurt out the *Yiddish* phrase "*Sheyn fergessen*," I forgot.

In *Yiddish*, "*Der kelner*" is the waiter; "*Di kelnerin*" is the waitress.

There's an amusing anecdote about the great novelist, Isaac Bashevis Singer. Singer loved automats. When he arrived in the United States from Poland in the 1930s, he sought out a "*restoran*" (restaurant). Wandering into an automat, he saw all the people carrying trays and thought, "What a wonderful country! One restaurant, and so many waiters!"

The *Yiddish* crosswords from the <u>Jewish Daily Forward</u> were a combination of *Yiddish* , Hebrew, and English words, according to Hal S. Barron, Professor of History. Appearing on the same page as the fabled "*Bintel Brief*," the <u>Forward</u>'s puzzles represented a mix of fun and English-language instruction. To help new immigrants learn English, the puzzles often gave clues in *Yiddish* and called for an answer that was an English word transliterated into Hebrew characters, such as the clue "*tsoris*," with the answer "*trouble*" written in Hebrew characters. At other times, the clue was in transliterated English and the answer in *Yiddish*, or both clue and answer were in the same language.

In January 2001, the Dora Teitelboim Center for *Yiddish* Culture and Florida International University jointly launched the first *Yiddish* on-line college program in the world.

The *Yiddish* expression, *"klaider machen dem mentshen"* means clothes make the man. One day in his office, Sen. Joe Lieberman was teased about whether he had accepted gifts of clothing from his supporters, as his colleague Sen. Robert Torricelli had allegedly. Sen. Lieberman rolled his eyes and said that he had bought the suit at a Brooks Brothers in Connecticut. "The salesman told me to look at the tag. It said, "Made in Israel." Unbelievable. Who ever heard of a suit made in Israel? Then he said, "Be careful with the pants. Those Israelis are a little short with the fabric."

Shelley Winters (Shirley Schrift), after two Oscars, four hit plays, and ninety-six films, describes her mother as "the source of my strength, talent, *chutzpah*, and ingenuity, and the lady I clung to no matter how many times I left home or got married."

Wilhelm Maurer said, "One well-known definition of *chutzpe* in Austria is as follows: *Chutzpe* has somebody who goes into the opera house wearing just a bathing suit, and deposits it at the wardrobe."

The *Yiddish* word for university is *"universitet."* Lawrence S. Bacow, president of Tufts University, said that the naming of a Jewish college president is hardly newsworthy anymore. MIT named Jerry Weisner as president in 1970, and since then Jewish presidents have reigned at prestigious institutions from Dartmouth to Harvard, Penn to Princeton. Formerly chancellor at MIT, Bacow sees a similarity. Both universities are *"haimishe places"*— not pretentious — and student-centered. Every door of the president's mansion on the Medford campus now hosts a *Mezzuzah*.

"Shmeykhl" or *"shmaichel"* is the *Yiddish* word for smile. According to Rav Yisroel Salanter, your face is a *"Reshut Harabim"* — a public domain. Everyone sees it, hence if you smile, it is encouraging and uplifting to others. If you were to frown (*"krimen zikh"*), then others who see you feel down and depressed (*"dershlogn"*). A smile is a LITTLE curve that sets A LOT of things straight.

"Sex, Love and Mistranslations on the *Yiddish* Stage," was a course offered at the YIVO institute for Jewish Research in Manhattan. The course description read, in part,

> Why do instances of prostitution, polygamy, and sexual promiscuity crop up in some of the earliest *Yiddish* plays? How do the same plays, call attention to the *Yiddish* language?

Katz's "operas" included Carmen Katz and The Barber of *Shlemiel*.

Mickey Katz (1909-1985) was a clarinetist, saxophonist, vocalist, conductor, and comedian. His revues, such as "*Borschtcapades*" and "*Farfel Follies*" established him permanently on the Borscht Belt. He was a master of parodies in song:

- Borscht Riders in the Sky
- How Much is That Pickle in the Window
- Don't Let the Schmaltz Get in Your Eyes
- I'm a Schlemiel of Fortune
- Moscovitz Ramble
- A Schmo is a Schmo
- Schleppin' My Baby Back Home
- Nature Bocher
- The Poiple Kishke Eater

———————◆———————

When Mickey Katz's parody of the American classic, "Home on the Range" ("*Haim Afen Range*") was introduced, in three days the stores around Times Square sold out the original 10,000 records and took orders for 25,000 more. The flip side was "*Yiddish* Square Dance," with Katz as an Arkansas hog caller.

———————◆———————

Professor Jeffrey Shandler wrote an article in YIVO Annual, vol. 20, 1991, in which he said that "In many of the English translations of Sholem Aleichem, certain *Yiddish* words or phrases are given in transcription, either with or without some kind of glossary. Although there are numerous such examples to be found throughout the canon, the items appearing in glossaries to Sholem Aleichem stories in English translation can be categorized thus:"

1. Words connected to Jewish ritual or scholarship: shoykhet, tales, sude, gemore, shul, etc. (the largest category).

2. Food words: farfl, tsimes, homentashn, grivn, tsholnt, etc.

3. Regional (not specifically Jewish) terminology: dacha, kopek, starosta, troyka, verst, kazatsky, etc.

4. *Yiddish* terms or expressions deemed untranslatable by virtue of their distinctive ethnic character: *luftmentsh, shlemil, shlimazl, gvald, lekhaym, mazltov, shnorer, goyisher kop*, etc.

"Chai-5" is a Klezmer group performing in Florida.

———————◆———————

Kirk Douglas ("The Ragman's Son — An Autobiography") said that during his elementary school days he had to make the transition from the broken *Yiddish*/English his parents spoke at home to the English spoken at school. The teacher asked him where his report card was, and he told her he left it in the *"almer"* — the pantry. *"Di shpayzkamer"* is also the *Yiddish* term for the pantry.

———————◆———————

The Italian says, "I'm tired and thirsty. I must have wine."

The Frenchman says, "I'm tired and thirsty. I must have cognac."

The Russian says, "I'm tired and thirsty. I must have beer."

The Mexican says, "I'm tired and thirsty. I must have tequila."

The Jew says, "I'm *farmatert* and *dorshtik*. I must have *tsukerkrenk* (diabetes)."

———————◆———————

Joel Siegel, Good Morning America film critic, said,

Even with my limited *Yiddish*, it took me less than two hours to come up with twenty-nine words for "schmuck." Not twenty-nine words for the male member . . . Twenty-nine ways to devalue our self-worth and describe the ironic and the literal joys and sorrows of human failure. They are:

Alter Kocker, Bonditt, Chazer, Farshtunkener, Kalike, Kvetch, Meeskeit, Mishugeh, Momzer, Nar, Nogoodnik, Noodge, Oomglick, Paskudnyak, Pisher, Putz, Schlong, Schmuck, Schnorrer, Schvantz, Shlemiel, Shlemazl, Shmegeggy, Shmendrick, Schmo, Schnook, Schtunk, Trombenik, Zhlob.

———————◆———————

A woman goes to *"der postamf"* (post office) to buy *"postgelt"* (postage) for her Chanukah cards. She says to *"der farkoyfer"* (clerk), "May I have hundert (100) Chanukah stamps?"
"What denomination?" says the clerk.
The woman says, "Oy vey, my G-d! Has it come to this? Okay. Give me *dreisik* (30) Orthodox, tzen (10) Conservative, *tzvontzik* (20) *Reform*, and *fertsik* (40) Reconstructionist."

The *Yiddish* term *"shleppost"* is sometimes used to represent the regular (nonelectronic) postal service.

"Ma. You're Gonna *Kvell* at This News" writes Gene Weingarten, the son and the [Washington Post] journalist to his dead mother, Ruth Weingarten, in Heaven.

"I know I never call or write, and I'm sorry. Ma. Today I'll make up for it. I've got news like you wouldn't believe. "No, Cousin Margaret did not finally arrive at an appointment on time. Some things are beyond the reach of man or God."

"Listen. They've picked a Jew to run on a national ticket. One heartbeat away, he would be. It's a fellow named Lieberman, of the Connecticut Liebermans."

"Yes, I know what you are thinking. You are thinking: Is it good for the Jews? No, Ma. I am not clairvoyant. You were always thinking: Is it good for the Jews?"

"Paper or plastic? You'd ask: Which is better for Israel? I know today's news worries you. Always, you worried when a Jewish person got too prominent. Because always you were afraid of one thing. A *shanda* for the *goyim*, you called it. You were afraid this person might mess up — a shame, a *shanda* — and when he did, all the non-Jews all over the world would point and say, "See? See how bad Jews are?" When Son of Sam turned out to be some *schiemiel* named Berkowitz, it nearly broke you. The Rosenberg's? I won't even go there. If you weren't already dead for Lewinsky, it would have killed you."

"Times have changed, Ma. We've come a long way since every Jew was seen as representing all Jews, and all had to measure up to some collective standard. Jews are like other people now. No longer do people named Jerome Levitch feel compelled to change their names to Jerry Lewis. One of the richest entertainers on earth today is named 'Jerry Seinfeld.' And yes, I know this worries you, too. You think that if Jerry Seinfeld is rich, then everyone will say, hey, those damned Jews have all the money!

"You are going to have to trust me on this one. This is good news, this Lieberman thing. Good for the country. Good for the Jews. 'Of course, if the Gore-Lieberman ticket loses, everyone will blame it on the Jew. Just kidding, Ma. Lighten up."

(Permission granted by Gene Weingarten at the Washington Post.)

A fax "mashin" at Bernstein-on-Essex-Street once received the following order: two wonton, one moo goo gai pan, one chow gai kow, two *rugelach*.

(Source: "The Book of Jewish Food" by Claudia Roden)

Marty Fiebert's Guide to Selective Yiddish Words and Phrases includes *"ungabluzim"* — to look as if one is going to cry.

The word *"kest"* refers to the practice of a man's supporting his new son-in-law for a year or two of study. According to Rabbi David E. Lipman,
> One of the ways to get ahead financially in the world was for a scholar to marry the daughter of a wealthy man. This gave status to the wealthy father by having a scholar as a son-in-law, and it enabled the son-in-law to study. The vast majority of our scholars began poor. Therefore, to survive, they married wives or families that could support them.

Is there an English word that is equivalent to *"kest"*?

According to Perets Mett (*Yiddish* Forum), this refers specifically to the young couple's taking their meals with the bride's parents for a specified period of time. In English, this is "board/boarding."

And Jack S. Berger says, "The process of providing a *Yeshivah bokhur* with meals was called '*essen teg.*' The idea was that the young man was fed on a daily basis, and may have rotated through a number of households. While 'boarding' makes sense for '*kest*,' I would opt for 'subsidized,' since I think it captures the spirit of what was happening a bit more closely."

The *Yiddish* dictionary, *"Kurtzer Yidish-Hebreyish-Rusisher Verterbuch"* by Yosef Guri and Shual [sic] Ferdman defines *"kest"* as *"hakhzakat he-khatan be-veit khotno"* — maintenance of the groom in the home of his father-in-law.

"Borscht" is defined as beet or cabbage soup. <u>Koshernosh.com</u> says that *"borscht"* has a more humorous definition: "A purple soup made from beets and ammonia. Always eaten by elderly Jews who slurp noisily."

Leo Burns asked Walter Matthau, "Hey, Walter, how come you belong to a tennis club and you don't play tennis?" Matthau's response: "They serve good *borscht* here."

"Goyisher nokhes" — as defined by Yetta Emmes — is pleasure from doing something traditionally un-Jewish, like hang gliding, auto racing, or entering a rural beer drinking contest.

Dick Capri, one of the Borscht Belt legends, calls himself "the token *goy*." Capri, an Italian Catholic, insists he feels Jewish. "I've worked for so many Jewish audiences, I'm on Schindler's list," said Capri.

---

1. What was said
2. What was thought by the hearer.
1. *Muter. Tate.* You know how you always said you might not always agree with what I did, but that you would still love me? Well, *es tut mir bahng.* Here's the thing. About der *oyto.*
2. Valium. I must have a Valium.

"Farges on dem valyum. Vi volt zikh gefirt bar-kokhba in dem?"

(Forget the Valium. How would the Lone Ranger handle this?)

A *"tummler,"* according to William Norwich, is *Yiddish* for "a fun maker, a catalyst, a jester." Mel Brooks, when interviewed for the <u>Las Vegas Weekly</u>, was asked, "When you were a child you had a job called a *Tummler*. What is a *tummler*?" He replied,

> A *Tummler* is an Americanization of a Jewish word. It comes from the Latin "Tumulet" which means chaos and excitement. A *Tummler* wakes up the Jews when they fall asleep around

the pool after lunch. He goes by and excites them and tells them jokes and stories. Instead of them drifting off, he keeps them happy and alert and that's his job. I was the pool *tummler.* One of the things I had to do as the pool *tummler* was I used to do an act. I wore a derby and an alpaca coat, and I would carry two rock-laden cardboard suitcases and go to the edge of the diving board and say, "Business is no good!" and jump off (laughs). Of course, my suitcases would take me right to the bottom; my derby would float on the surface. I was looking up at the blond, gentile lifeguard who would have mercy. Dive down and save me (laughs).

Joseph Dorinson says, "A *tummler* is *Yiddish* for 'fool or noisemaker who does anything and everything to entertain the customers so that they won't squawk about their rooms or food.' "

BorschtBelt.net says Mal Z. Lawrence, King of Catskill comedy, is known as a "*tumult-maker.*" His middle initial, Z, stands for "Elliott." He has a French poodle named *"Zeesah" (Yiddish* for sweet).

Leon H. Gildin says that a *"tummler"* is a noisemaker; if Buddy Hackett is at your party, you've definitely got one.

Patricia A. Weiner ("Reminiscing: The Catskills in the '50s") wrote about Lou Goldstein (at Grossingers), fondly called "Uncle Lou," but known in the trade as a social director, or *tummler . . .* Every big hotel had its own *tummler*, and it was his job to keep the action going.

"*Kumzitz,*" according to Miriam Weinstein ("*Yiddish — A Nation of Words*") is defined as two separate words meaning "come', and "sit."

A *"Kumzitz"* — The Shmooze Cafe, is an activity of the Workmen's Circle/Arbeter Ring of Michigan. Ellen Bates-Brackett, director, says that *"Kumzitz"* is like a salon, with intellectual and philosophical discussions on compelling topics, accompanied by readings. The meetings are held in private homes.

Howard Simons ("<u>Jewish Times — Voices of the American Jewish Experience</u>") defines *"komsitz"* as an informal get-together.

Aaron Ninedek ("<u>*Nudnik's* Tales</u>") has penned some wonderful stories of his early experiences in Betar camps in Australia and also while at the "Machon" in Jerusalem (AKA "HaMachon LeMadrichel Chutz La Aretz"). He wrote:

"Kum. Zitz. Ess a Bissel!" I sometimes thought that this must have been another way of saying "Hello! How are you?" in *Yiddish* because it was the way elderly Jewish ladies greeted you when you visited them. When I would reply, "Fine. Thank you!" they would make me sit down and they would start to feed me.

I could speak *Yiddish*, so I knew that *"Kum. Zitz. Ess a Bissell"* actually meant, "Come. Sit. Eat a little!" Of course, "Eat a Little" in *Yiddish* means keep eating until you burst.

At the Machon, when we heard that there was to be a *Kumzitz*, it had nothing to do with elderly Jewish ladies, but could be relied upon to include a number of young, attractive ones. A *Kumzitz* generally came soon after food parcels arrived from home, because these always included real Nescafe . . . stir this paste with some vigor until it becomes whitish and a little frothy. Add hot water, and HEAVEN!!"

"Der rak" means "the cancer," according to Herman Galvin and Stan Tamarkin ("<u>The *Yiddish* Dictionary Sourcebook: A Transliterated Guide to the *Yiddish* Language</u>"). Fran Drescher was diagnosed with cancer; subsequently she wrote a book titled, "<u>Cancer Schmancer</u>."

Dee Anthony (Michael Mulheren), the newly-hired manager for Peter Allen (Hugh Jackman) in the Broadway show, "<u>The Boy From Oz</u>," uses three *Yiddish* words: *"shtup," "putz"* and *"shmuck."*

In the book, "<u>MitzvahChic</u>" by Gail Greenberg, there are chapters titled, "The Torah for the *Farchadat*" and another called "Eight Complete Parties That Will Leave You *Farklempt*."

The *Schlemiel-schlimazel* duality has been amply documented. According to Joseph Dorinson, the *schlimiel* is just clumsy. He drops bread on the floor. The *schlimazel* also drops the bread on the floor . . . but with buttered side down.

A *schlemiel*, according to <u>WordNet 2.0 Vocabulary Helper</u>, is defined as follows:

- "space cadet"— someone who seems unable to respond appropriately to reality (as if under the influence of some narcotic drug).
- "square lame" — someone who doesn't understand what is going on.
- "sheep" — a timid defenseless simpleton who is readily preyed upon.
- (*Yiddish*) a dolt who is a habitual bungler.

Baruch Podolsky (<u>*Yiddish* Forum</u>) shared the following proverb: *"Af morgn zol got zorgn"* — About tomorrow God should care (not me). The English equivalent: Cross the bridge when you come to it. The preposition "af" is usually spelled "oyf" — alef-vov-yud-langer fey, but the common pronunciation is "af."

Marcia Gruss Levinsohn (alias *"bobe mashinke"*) wrote *"Di dray bern, mirele goldherele antshuldikt zikh"* — The Three Bears, Goldylocks Apologizes. The book starts:

"*Es iz nosh hashone. Der zeyde zitst in shul. Un dos eynikl iz gekumen tsu gast.*"

(It is Rosh Hashone. Grandfather is at Synagogue services. And a grandchild has come to visit.)

After the section depicting a traditional telling of the story, Mirele returns, with her *Zeyde*, to the three bears and apologizes, bringing apples and honey. The *Zeyde* fixes the chair she had broken.

"*Shiksa* Goddess Blintzes Kugel", is a recipe contained in "<u>Kona Beth Shalom's Shaloha Cookbook</u>."

"Potchkey," according to Yetta Emmes, means to fuss with or mess up. When you *potchkey,* you end up making a mishmash.

Judge Judy Sheindlin said [of her TV show], "The pay is good. I get someone to *patshkey* with my face so I look good."

"Der musey" is Yiddish for the museum. The Lower Last Side Tenement Museum is located at 90 Orchard Street. The tenement house, built in 1863, is unchanged from the time when "der imigrant" families crowded its *"fintster"* (dark), unsavory apartments, devoid of baths. The interiors of *"finf"* apartments were recreated with period furnishings, as well as family mementos and photos.

Many years ago The Pillsbury Company's ads for flour said, "For Your Sabbath Chollah." Borden's homogenized milk advertised, *"Buba* never dreamed of such milk!"

The theme song of the sitcom, "Laverne and Shirley" was titled, "Making Our Dreams Come True." The opening lines: "One, two, three, four, five, six, seven, eight, *Schlimiel, schlimazel, hasenpfeffer,* incorporated."

Maxpages.com gives the following definition for *"Feh":*

Feh: There really is no translation for *"feh."* The closest you might come is "p'shaw!" It is used to express disbelief or disgust. *"Feh!"* is so expressive that when it is used, no further explanation is generally required, such as: (upon hearing that someone you hate has just been awarded the Nobel Peace Prize). *"Feh!"* (upon hearing that your wonderful son the doctor has been sued for malpractice). *"Feh!"* (upon hearing that Congress has awarded itself yet another pay raise). *"Feh!"* You get the idea.

Butler Library In New York City houses the History of the *Yiddish* Atlas Project and tape recordings of the stories of *Yiddish*-speaking Holocaust survivors, documented by Marvin Herzog.

Dr. Vosef Guri's book, "All's Well That Ends Well," is a collection of proverbs in four languages: English, Russian, *Yiddish* and Hebrew. It was published in Jerusalem. One of his proverbs:

"A volf farlirt zayne hor, ober nit zayn natur."

Compare: A leopard cannot change his spots.

Joseph Aaron (Chicago Jewish News) composed a list of his favorite Jewish things (with apologies to "The Sound of Music"). They included:

Potato *kugel*

Latkes

Kvelling when a prominent Jew does something to bring pride to the Jewish people.

Chicken soup. Go ahead, make joke, but I love the stuff, can't get enough. As long as it's made by my mother.

The faces of *bubbies* and *zaydies*.

A beautifully-designed *ketubah*.

Saying kaddish on my father's *yahrzeit*.

Chuppahs.

A heartfelt, personal eulogy that captures the essence of the departed.

A *mensch*.

Kishke. Preferably swimming in gravy.

The large number of words like *shlep, kvetch* and the ever-popular *tush* that you hear on late-night TV talk shows.

A *fahrbrengen*. If you don't know what that is, call your nearest Lubavitch Chabad House and ask them to invite you to the next one they have.

Hearing American songs sung with *Yiddish* words. I could listen to the *Yiddish* version of "Fiddler on the Roof" and to Mandy Patinkin singing "Take Me Out to the Ballgame" in *Yiddish* for hours on end.

A *"mensch"* is a person of good character — a kid who doesn't embarrass his parents and behaves well, according to Dan Sharon, head librarian, Asher Library at Spertus Institute of Jewish Studies.

Joseph Aaron wrote an article titled, "Joys of Jewish." He wrote,

I absolutely love *Yiddish.*

But there is a *Yiddish* phrase, one of the best known of all *Yiddish* phrases, that I absolutely hate.

"*Shver tsan a Yid.*" It's hard to be a Jew.

He concludes, No, it is not *shver tsan a Yid.* It is anything but. There is so much going on in the Jewish world, so many ways to connect to the Jewish world, so many paths in the Jewish world, an avenue no matter what your interest and something that feels better then anything for it is most authentically you.

No reason to *kvetch,* so many reasons to *kvell.*

It's great to be a Jew.

A *"mensch"* takes the blame for when they're wrong, keeps a promise to their mother, does things that are inconvenient because they're the right thing to do. It's an endangered species, says Neil Steinberg, columnist for the <u>Chicago Sun-Times</u>.

State Rep. Jeff Schoenberg sees the *mensch* question in largely political terms. He said,

". . . Sen. Joe Lieberman is the prototype *mensch.* I've had the opportunity to spend time with him, and in his personal qualities, he exhibits a level of integrity and other qualities that transcend partisanship."

Other political *mensches,* according to Schoenberg, are former Sen. Paul Simon and his late wife, Jeanne; recently deceased longtime congressman, Sid Yates; former congressman, federal judge and White House counsel, Abner Mikva, who helped Schoenberg get started in politics; and a Republican *mensch,* just retired Rep. John Porter.

The University of Indiana — hardly located in the center of Jewish culture — has an endowed chair in *Yiddish* Studies. You can study *Yiddish* at the University of Illinois at Chicago, at Spertus Institute of Jewish Studies, at the Dawn Schuman Institute, or with a private instructor.

The <u>Chicago Jewish News</u> ran a weekly quiz testing your Jewish IQ. Questions 70-79 asked, "How's Your *Yiddish*?"

70. *balebos* — the person in charge. Literally, master of the house.

71. *kochleffel* — one who is always getting involved. Literally, a cooking spoon.

72. *frailech* — joyful.

73. *mishpoche* — family, extended family.

74. *mameloshen* — mother tongue. *Yiddish*.

75. *shoyn fargessen* — I forgot already!

76. *yichus* — family connections.

77. *shver tzu zein a Yid* — it's hard to be a Jew.

78. *zei gezunt* — be well, be healthy.

79. *bubba meisses* — stories of little value. Literally, grandmother stories.

———————◆———————

Word historian, Martha Barnette, defines the word *"chochkuh"* (also spelled *"tsatske," "tsatskeleh," "chachka,"* and *"chotchke"*) as follows: It comes from *Yiddish*, and made its first recorded appearance in English during the 1960s. It means an inexpensive trinket, bauble, or ornament.

She defines the word *"kibitz"* as follows:

1. To look on and offer unsolicited, meddlesome advice.

2. To chat or make wisecracks (especially when others are trying to work or have a serious conversation).

Ms. Barnette says, "This handy *Yiddishism* derives from a picturesque German source: In German, the verb *kiebitzen* means 'to look on while other people are playing cards' (especially if it's done annoyingly, like standing too close).

Even more picturesque, this verb derives from German *Kiebitz*, the name of a type of little bird that has a reputation for being particularly noisy and inquisitive.

———————◆———————

The theme song of <u>The Yiddish Voice</u> (WUNR 1600 AM, Brookline, Massachusetts) is *"lomir ale in eynem"* (let's all get together).

Kenneth Jones wrote a review of Jeremy Kareken's play, *"Farblondjet,"* which takes its title from the *Yiddish* for "all mixed up." He wrote,

> *Farblondjet* shows the story of a young man as he looks for love amongst the ruins of a dying civilization, the Jewish Catskills. There, he finds the one love he can not have, the father he never liked, and a whole lot of *tsuris, michagas,* and maybe a *shtup* or two.

According to David Fox, the third-generation owner of the Fox's U-Bet Chocolate-Flavored Syrup Company, the secret ingredient in egg creams is Brooklyn's *"vaser."* Who invented egg creams? No one knows for sure. One story credits the *Yiddish* actor, Boris Thomashevsky, "America's Darling." Supposedly, Boris had enjoyed a similar drink in Paris and when he came to New York, he tried to duplicate it and that's how the famous New York egg cream was born.

Yiddish writer, Isaac Bashevis Singer had the following to say about the language in his 1978 Nobel Prize acceptance speech:

> *Yiddish* language — a language of exile, without a land, without frontiers, not supported by any government, a language which possesses no words for weapons, ammunition, military exercises, war tactics . . . There is a quiet humor in *Yiddish* and a gratitude for every day of life, every crumb of success, each encounter of love. The *Yiddish* mentality is not haughty. It does not take victory for granted. It does not demand and command but it muddles through, sneaks by, smuggles itself amidst the powers of destruction, knowing somewhere that God's plan for Creation is still at the very beginning . . . In a figurative way, *Yiddish* is the wise and humble language of us all, the idiom of frightened and hopeful Humanity.

Contrary to what Isaac Bashevis Singer said, Hershl Hartman defines the following military terms:

weapons — *gever, kley-zayin, vofn*
ammunition — *amunitsye;* (obs.: *voyener zapas*)
military exercises — *militerishe ibungen genitungen;*
   (obs.: *soldatn mushtir*)
war tactics — *milkhome taktik;* (obs.: *krigs-Listikeyt*)

According to Richard F. Shepard and Vicki Gold Levi ("<u>Live & Be Well — A Celebration Of Yiddish Culture In America</u>"),

> The great source of Sholem Aleichem's material was his open door — which he advertised in *Yiddish* newspapers — inviting in anyone who cared to speak with him. His daughter, Marie Waife-Goldberg, wrote that some of his visitors were bores, "but others had information to offer, what America was like, how people lived here, and the stories of their own experience in the land of Columbus." My father absorbed it all in amazement.

Alex Berger (<u>The Times Ledger Newspapers</u>) wrote a review of the off-Broadway musical, "<u>A Stoop on Orchard Street</u>." The piece was titled, "A Stoop On Orchard Street is *oysgetsayche.*" His comments:

> Despite the minor discrepancies, I found "Stoop" to be *"oysgetsaychen"* (outstanding) and *"unterhaltunk"* (good entertainment). If you liked "<u>Fiddler On The Roof</u>," you'll love "<u>A Stoop On Orchard Street</u>." It continues where "<u>Fiddler On The Roof</u>" leaves off.

"Es is shver tzu makhen a lebel" means "It's hard to make a living; it's hard to make ends meet." Mikhoyel Basherives (<u>Yiddish Forum</u>) said,

> *"Makhn a lebn"* is American *Yiddish*. Friends who grew up in Europe have laughed when hearing it. The closest to the American phrase in *Yiddish* everywhere else is *"Fardinen zikh dos lebn. Hobn fun vos tsu lebn* (aside from *Hobn parnose,* etc.).

When Molly Picon was 51, she did a program for Rokeach Soap. The first show consisted of her singing some songs in *Yiddish* and English. Everyone seemed to like her, except Rokeach. They wanted no *Yiddish*. After the second show, they changed their minds . . . and their shows got better.

"Tshemadon" is a suitcase or sample case, and *"tshemadonikle"* is an attaché case.

"Der begazh" is *Yiddish* for the baggage. *"Hekel pekel"* also means bag and baggage. Molly Picon wrote that in 1943 she was offered a job in Hollywood, and she and Yonkel left hastily, *"heckel pekel"*, (bag and baggage).

———————◆———————

Will Shortz, editor of the <u>New York Times</u> puzzle, checked the crossword database at <u>www.cruciverb.com</u>, which contains the clues and answers for 7-8 leading American crosswords, going back to 1997. He found that the most-used *Yiddish* word in crosswords is *NOSH*, which (together with its various forms *NOSHES, NOSHED,* and *NOSHER*) turned up in 57 puzzles. The next most common *Yiddish* words were *YENTA,* with 43 appearances, and *SCHMO/ SHMO,* with 37.

Then, in descending order:
> *GELT* — 21
> *SCHLEP/SHLEP* — 15
> *TOV* (as part of the phrase *"Mazel tov"*) — 15
> *OYS* (plural of the exclamation) — 9
> *GOLEM* — 7
> *KIBITZ/KIBBITZ* — 4
> *MENSCH* — 4
> *SCHTICK/SHTICK* — 4
> *GANEF* — 3
> *TSURIS* — 3
> *KVETCH* — 2
> *SCHLOCK* — 2
> *SCHMALTZ* — 2
> *KVELL* — 1
> *SCHLEMIEL* — 1
> *SCHNOZ* — 1

Mr. Shortz said, "As a crossword editor, I love to see familiar *Yiddish/ English* words in crosswords, because they're so expressive and their letter patterns are different from those of most other English vocabulary."

———————◆———————

"Matzo dramas," according to Harry Sapoznik, were radio dramas that were sponsored by the Manishewitz Matzo Company. "There was no *Yiddish* Lone Ranger. There was no *Yiddish* Buck Rodgers. The *Matzo dramas* dealt with such vital issues of the day as assimilation, intergenerational conflict, labor strife and the clash between religious and secular life for American Jews," said Sapoznik.

"The *Kvetch* of the Goddess" (author unknown) said, in part:

Come, *kinderlech*, come, *nosh a bissel*, sit and listen to your Mama, She Who Knows Best — what do you mean, why do I know best? Because I'm your mother, that's why! Now sit and listen, after all the aggravation I've had with you! *Oy!* But you're a good kid, so I don't mind all the *tsoris*. Of course, it would help if you were going to school for a real degree . . .

Now where was I? *Oy* yes, you're meeting in some *verkuckte* God forsaken place no one has heard [of] and you have to spend an hour trying to find the right street to turn onto, and when you get there you still aren't sure if this is the right place because everyone else is even more *verblondjet* than you are, and won't show up for another hour anyway. But you get there, you're patient, you learned it from me, I admit, and when you are all together you have a *nosh*, you sing, you have a *nosh*, you dance — not these strange newfangled dances with that trashy music, but good music, like we had when I was your age — you have a *nosh*, you meet a nice person and do what you want, but I don't want to know about it; just be careful. I don't need a grandchild that badly — well I do, come to think of it, you're not getting any younger you know, and when are you going to meet someone, please?! And whatever you do, don't do anything that people will talk about; you know those nosy neighbors. And don't worry about me, I'll be home waiting up for you; stay as late as you want, I'll be okay by myself . . . I don't need to go out and have fun; I'm not a spring chicken anymore, after all. Which reminds me, the doctor says I need to watch my cholesterol. Do you know any good diet books? . . . Just a little peace and quiet is all I ask from you, and maybe you can settle down finally and give me a grandchild? I'm not getting any younger, you know. I would like to see a grandchild before I move to Sun City or Century Village. Is that too much for your mother to ask? No?

———————◆———————

"*A Glezele Tay*" is a glass of tea.

"*A Glezele Tay mit tzuker*" is a glass of tea with a sugar cube held between the teeth.

"*A Glezele Tay mit varenya*" is a glass of tea with cherry preserves.

"*Tai mit limeneh*" is a tea with lemon.

Dr. Howard Markel wrote, "After decades of toil and struggle, multiple college degrees, other significant achievements, and the birth and growth of children and grandchildren into adulthood, suddenly we are talking about the 'good old days' with our *bubbehs* over a glass of tea."

Mark Altman is the curator of the *"Glezele Tey"* series at the Folksbiene *Yiddish* Theatre in Manhattan. He wishes to extend a *bisl heymishkayt* to the public by offering a series of artists, of all sorts, interacting in a warm environment.

"Kibitzer" was the title of a [1929] play by Jo Swerling.

"Farbrent," according to the Pittsburgh Jewish Community Center's Glossary of Terms means "as burning; zealous." *"Farbrenen"* means to burn, and *"faver"* is fire.

Mickey Katz used the word *"farbrent"* in his novelty records:

Sixteen tons all kinds smoked fishes,
Latkes, blintzes un heyse [hot] knishes,
O Lordy nem es shnell [take me quickly] to the promised land!
A fayer afn boss zol er vern farbrent!
[a fire on the boss, may he get burned up!]

On Saturday Night Live, Linda Richman said, "I'm getting a little emotional. I'm getting *farklempt* . . . talk amongst yourselves . . . I'll give you yet another topic: Franklin Delano Roosevelt's New Deal was neither new nor a deal. Discuss. There, I feel better."

Howard Simons wrote about his experiences as a waiter in the Catskills. A lady wanted a *"linkesveal."* Not wishing to appear rude or dumb, he went into the kitchen and shouted to the Chinese chef. "One *linkesveal.*" Out it comes — a lean piece of veal. He also remembers one women at breakfast, who said, "*Vaiter.* I vant a ricekrips mitot milk." Simons said, "Lady, do you mean with hot milk or without milk?" She says, "That's right, *mitot* milk." (So he brought the milk on the side.)

Jackie Mason advertised tickets to his Broadway musical review, "Laughing Room Only" by saying, "I'm offering 25% off all performances through Dec. 24, 2003. Don't be a *shmuck*, hurry before all of the tickets are gone!"

On the TV series, "Whoopi," Whoopi Goldberg (Mavis Rae) told Wren T. Brown (Courtney Rae), "Courtney, you are my brother and I love you, but you're a *shmuck*."

Michael Wex (author of "*Shlepping the Exile*") is a *lamed-vovnik* of humor. He says that sarcasm in *Yiddish* has its own flavor. "A good *Yiddish* curse is open-ended. It leaves the person who gets cursed to do the real work," says Wex. For instance, being told in *Yiddish*, "Doctors should need you, tends to linger a lot longer than telling someone to drop dead."'

Wex insists that a *Yiddish* insult can also be a compliment. "It depends on the intelligence of the person getting cursed. You take the *Yiddish* comment home with you and think about it for a long time."

The Kressyn-Rexite (Seymour Rexite and Miriam Kressyn) concoctions struck big with American Jews. Kressyn's translations pleased listeners. Ex.

"love and marriage"
geyt tzuzamen vi zup un knaydlakh
(go together like soup and *knaydlakh*)

It was in the *Yiddish* theater that the late Seymour Rexite had his greatest success. He starred in "*Dem Rebbens Nigun*" ("The Rabbi's Melody"), and "*Dos Yidishe Maydele*" ("The Jewish Girl"). He appeared in one of the first full-length *Yiddish* films with sound, "*Mayn Yidishe Mame*" ("My Jewish Mother") in 1930 and in the *Yiddish* film, "*Motl der Operator*" ("Motl the Operator").

Ruth Wisse is Harvard's first professor of *Yiddish* literature. She assumed this position in 1993.

There's a *Yiddish* proverb: "God could not be everywhere, so He made mothers." In *Yiddish*: "*Got hot nish gekent zayn iberal, hot er bashafen mames.*"

———————◆———————

In 2003, the 78th Street Theatre Lab in Manhattan presented Mark Zeller's comedy, "*Schmaltz.*" Their Press Release read:

> ". . . *SCHMALTZ* is a hilarious romp through the neuroses of a man on a quest for enlightenment and nourishment. In the middle of a mid-life crisis, Benny is unhappy, unhealthy and hungry for the comfort foods of his childhood: Gefilte fish with horseradish on Challah bread, egg creams and chicken fat sandwiches. In an attempt to lift Benny's mood — and lower his cholesterol — his wife Trina puts him into a hypnotic trance that puts him face-to-face with family and food. It's chicken fat sandwiches for the soul."

———————◆———————

Michael Toscano of the Washington Post, reviewed the show, "*OY!*" He said, "If you know the lyrics to the Andrews Sisters' hit '*Bei Mir Bist DeSchoen,*' then *OY!* is the *schmear* you want for your bagels."

———————◆———————

Since 1979, Portlanders have enjoyed the Sunday morning Yiddish Hour, hosted by Jack "Yankl" Falk, Reva Falk, Amy Shapiro and Jeff Olenick. They feature a wide selection of traditional and contemporary Jewish music: klezmer, chassidic, cantorial, *Yiddish* and Israeli theatre and folk, Mizrahi pop, Ladino, Jewish classical, Yeshiva rock, Judeo-Arabic, and more.

———————◆———————

According to Leo Lieberman, "A *shmateh* is what your husband's second wife wears."

———————◆———————

Jackie Mason says that "A *shmatte* to a wife is also everything her husband is wearing. It's most often used after the husband gets dressed. No matter what he's got on, she says, You're not ashamed to walk down the street with a *shmatte* like that! Is that all you have to put on? What, you don't care?"

Source: "How To Talk Jewish"
by Jackie Mason with Ira Berkow.

An unidentified reader won Honorable Mention in <u>New York Magazine's</u> Competition Number 754 with the following near-miss name:

> Ernst *Lubavitch* — master of Hasidic farce; e.g., "The Shul Around the Corner," "Ninoytchka.'"

"*A Brivele der Mamen*" ("<u>A Letter to Mother</u>," 1939) is one of the last *Yiddish* films made before the Nazi invasion of Poland.

Bernstein-on-Essex-Street (now out of business and not to be confused with "Essex on Coney" in Brooklyn), once sponsored a writing competition for sayings to be put into fortune cookies. Among the winners:

> "If wishes were knishes, every *shnorer* would be fat."

Peter Hupalo coined the word "*menschkins*" (not to be confused with the little "Munchkins" in the <u>Wizard of Oz</u>.) He writes that "*menschkins*" don't really want to help a person a lot for fear the person will outdo them, but fear if they do not help at least a little bit, they will have no future store of goodwill in case the person becomes the next eGodImRich.com founder.

"*Verklempt*," according to <u>Urbandictionary.com</u>, is fake *Yiddish* for "overcome with emotion" and comes from the Linda Richman skits on <u>Saturday Night Live</u>. A second definition: being overcome with emotion, usually not of joy, but rather emotions that hurt. As an emotional heartache.

Brigitte Dayan, *JUF News*, remembers the late Gene Siskel (the master movie critic) as a "*mensch*." Steven Nasalin, Chicago JUF/ Jewish Federation president, said,

> "In an era when public figures often have little to do with their community, Gene was a *mensch* whose Judaism was paramount in his life and who was a very willing and active member of his community."

"Vershtickt" means choking or gagging. It's the feeling you get when cleaning your freezer after a long power outage.

"Tsimes" is a vegetable or fruit stew; a big deal (slang). *"Makh nit keyn tsimes fun dem"* means "Don't make a fuss about it." (Don't make a fruit stew from it.) Red Buttons once said, "My father loved to clown . . . The *tsimmes* doesn't fall too far from the tree."

According to Alan Mendelson, *"Yiddish* For the Presidential Campaign" (Moredeals.com), "Politicians and their wives will be careful to wear nice *shmatahs* while they're on the campaign trail to impress the world with good taste, but not fancy designer *shmatahs* that could alienate some voters."

"Di tsatske" — a toy or trinket — was the subject of an article by Margaret Webb Pressler, a Washington Post staff writer. In her piece titled, "But Spending Is a Holiday Ball," she wrote, "Retailers certainly make it easy to rack up the gifts at this time of year, too, with strategically placed displays of cute little *tchotchkes* and whatnots."

Ronnie Caplan wrote a piece for the Jewish Bulletin of North Carolina titled, "Jews in Fashion? Should we break out the Manischewitz?" She wrote,

> "And Lieberman is bringing Jewish humor to what would have been an otherwise boring campaign. Like his proposed campaign slogans 'With malice toward none but a little guilt for everyone,' or 'Ask not what your country can do for you, ask what you can do for your mother.' "

The Workmen's Circle is the oldest existing *Yiddish* chorus in the country.

"Feigelah Schmeygelah," was the title of a (1999) Evening of Queer Jewish humor, performed in San Francisco.

Barbra Streisand has been sprinkling *Yiddish* words throughout her films, her music, and in interviews. Here's a compilation courtesy of Newsletter/BarbraFile.com, Allison J. Waldman, publisher:

"fabrent" — Vanity Fair (1991)
"I always had extraordinary willpower . . . My grandmother used to call me *fabrent*, which means on fire. I just couldn't accept no for an answer. I still can't."

"fekakte" — Vanity Fair (1994)
"What's Whitewater compared to Watergate? At worst it's some 10 year-old *fekakte* real-estate deal."

"geyshrey" — Playboy interview (1977)
"Sometimes when I hear that first record of mine, where I'm *geshreying* and getting so emotional, I think, 'Oh, God, how did they ever like me?! I'm embarrassed by it."

"gonif" — Thief
In Funny Lady, when Billy takes Fanny's cigarette case and forget to return it, she asks for it back. He gives it to her and she murmurs derisively, "*Gonif.*"

"gonza megillah" — In her Washington stop of The Concert, Barbra used the expression when talking about the media.

"I must admit that I was a little afraid to come back here after the *gonza megillah* the press made over my visit to Washington last year. *Gonza megillah* sounds like a Japanese movie, but it's *Yiddish* for 'big deal.' "

"meeskite" — In The Concert, Barbra looks at the photo of herself at age 13 and says, "What a *meeskite.*"

"mensch" — In an interview with Barbara Walters (1985), Barbra was asked about her son, Jason. She answered, "He's a *mensh.*"

"mishegoss" — In a (1977) Playboy interview, Barbra talks about being in group therapy. "I'm finding out about life, talking to people, hearing what they feel and think. They've got the same *meshegoss* I do; it has nothing to do with my being an actress."

"nu" — In "Second Hand Rose," Barbra sings, ". . . from Second Avenue, *nu*?"

"pupik" — In a (1993) interview, with Barbara Walters on 20/20, Barbra describes her shooting The Prince of Tides. Barbra explains, "there were days we were filming and I was up to my *pupik* in the water."

"tchotchkes" — In <u>Look</u> (1969), Barbra talks about her thrift shop goodies, her art works, and her favorite things: "I'm a slave to all my *tchotchkes.*"

The word *"tchotchkes"* is used by Michael Northrop in his weather terms:

> Small craft advisory alerts mariners to the presence of sustained weather, sea conditions, or *tchotchkes* either present or forecast, that can be potentially hazardous or decorative to small boats.

The Style invitational, Week 530, in <u>The Washington Post</u>, asked readers to take a word and alter it in three ways by adding a letter, changing a letter, and deleting a letter and supply definitions for the resulting three words. Here were some of the winning entries:

Mohel
Maohel — a famous Chinese circumciser, discredited for his disastrous great lop forward;

Ohel — What you don't want to hear the rabbi say during the procedure;

Aohel — An Internet provider notorious for its painful service cutoffs.

— Grendan Beary

Zaftig
Aftig — Having a pleasingly plump behind;

Zaftpig — Past the point of pleasingly plump;

Daftig — Fat AND stupid.

— Tom Witte

A *"Matzoh Ball"* (MAWT.suh bawl), according to Mitch Wagner, is a Jewish party or dance held on Christmas Eve, or Christmas Day. Also: *Matzo Ball.* Wagner said that his brother, Adam, told him that it was traditional to hold Christmas Eve parties among Jewish singles living in Manhattan in the 1990s — after all, the following day was a day off from work. The parties were for Jews because Christians were assumed to be with their families on Christmas Eve.

Adam Sandler has a bulldog named *"Matzo Ball."*

"A *yingerer oylem"* is a younger audience; "An *elterer oylem"* is an older audience.

Cindy Adams reported that "if someone falls out of a chair (*"shtul"*) laughing at the Folksbien *Yiddish* Theater comedy, 'The Lady Next Door,' it's normally a good thing. At one performance, it was not a good thing. Two dozen wheelchair customers from a nursing home were in the house. One lady who wasn't laughing just fell out of her chair. She wasn't hurt. Allen Rickman, the theater's director, said, "We're trying to appeal to a younger audience — like people in their 50s. This doesn't help."

Comedian Phil Carr, used to come to the Catskills with his *"zun."* His son would read the Lincoln Gettysburg Address, and Phil would do a literal translation into *Yiddish.* It began: Four score and seven years ago, *"Efsher, ziben ochztik yohr tsurecht, undzer fier tates,* our four fathers, ..."

Billy Hodes, another comic in the Mountains, did the *"essen"* bit:

You come up to the Mountains. You go to the hotel. "The dining room is open." And the band would play, *"Essen, mir gayn essen. Essen, mir gayn fressen."* Hey waiter, loverboy from the bushes, I want some orange juice, tomato juice. He went through the whole menu. He [the guest] ordered everything on the menu. Then they go outside and sit on the porch — on a rocking chair — "Mir rocken S." "How long are you here for?" "I'm here for tzvay voks (three weeks). "Oh, yeah. I'm here for the whole season." And then you hear an announcement, and the trumpet player had to go "Ba-da-bump-ba-da, bump-ba-da." And they said, "The dining room is open for lunch." "Essen, mir gayn essen. Essen, mir gayn fressen."

(Thanks to Pete Sokolow)

According to Darryl Lyman ("The Jewish Comedy Catalog"), Fanny Brice (Fannie Borach), comedienne, could not speak or understand *Yiddish*. In her skits, she adopted a *Yiddish*-English accent and would come on stage in a Madame Dubarry pompadour wig and proclaim with a heavy *Yiddish* accent, "I'm a bad *vomen*, but I'm good company."

A *"talis"* is a Jewish prayer shawl. Several websites carried this joke in English, but it's even funnier when *Yiddish* words are substituted:

"*Di aeroplan*" (airplane) was about to crash. There were *"finf"* (five) passengers on board but only *"fir"* (four) parachutes. The first passenger said, "I'm Kobe Bryant, the best NBA basketball player. The Lakers need me; I can't afford to die." So he took the *"ershter"* (first) pack and left the plane. The second passenger, Hillary Clinton, said, "I am *"di froy"* (the wife) of the former President of the United States. I am also the most ambitious woman in *"di velt"* (the world) and I am a "Noo Yawk" Senator and a potential future president." She just took the *"tsveyter"* (second) parachute and jumped out of the plane. The third passenger, George W. Bush, said, "I'm President of the United States of America. I have a great responsibility being the leader of a superpower nation. And above all, I'm the cleverest President in American History so America's people won't let me die." So he put on the pack next to him and jumped out of the plane. The *"ferter"* (fourth) passenger, an elderly gentleman, says to the *"finfter"* (fifth) passenger, a Rabbi, "I am old and frail and I don't have many years left. I will sacrifice my life and let you have the *"letst"* (last) parachute." The Rabbi said, "It's OK. There's a parachute left for you. America's cleverest President has just taken my *talis* bag."

Leonard Nimoy (Mr. Spock), the son of a Ukrainian-born barber, grew up speaking *Yiddish* in a one-bedroom apartment shared by six relatives in Boston's West End, a Jewish enclave in the predominantly Catholic city. His knowledge of the *mamaloshen* helped him land roles with visiting *Yiddish* theater troupes. Nimoy once had an appointment for an audition with legendary star, Maurice Schwartz. While waiting for Schwartz to acknowledge him, he heard his wife say in *Yiddish*, "He looks like the gentile in 'It's Hard to be a Jew." (She didn't know that Nimoy spoke the language.)

Saul Reichlin, who starred in the show "Sholom Aleichem: Now You're Talking," said that some of the charm of the original [Sholom Aleichem] tales is lost in the translation. I was lucky to find a good translation, but there is not a language in the world like *Yiddish*. 'Oh dear' is not funny, but you only need to say '*Oh veh*,' and people start laughing."

Reichlin gave an example of the difference between English and *Yiddish* in translation:

"An art critic might write, in English, 'This artist is insufficiently equipped technically and creatively to undertake a work of any real quality.' In *Yiddish* this translates as: 'They should chop his hands off.' "

———————◆———————

There are two words for potato in *Yiddish*: *"bulve"* and *"kartofl."*

———————◆———————

According to Philip Kutner, there are less than 500 people in the U.S. who either are currently teaching *Yiddish* or have ever taught a *Yiddish* class. This statement applies to the non-Chassidic community, and does not include the Chassidic teachers.

———————◆———————

Peter Gorin (Sillymusic.com) wrote,

Yiddish is probably the most expressive language in the world. So many of the words give away their meaning just by their sound. For instance, that gutteral "ch" sound as in Chaloshes. Does any word that means something good start with this sound? Don't tell me Challah, because that's a much softer sound. As a matter of fact, does any word that has that sound anywhere mean something good? Face it. How can you be saying something good by saying a word that you practically have to spit in order to pronounce properly? How about that. "kl" sound, as in *Fahklumpt*, *fahklempt* . . . not such a good thing!

———————◆———————

The *"Say Oy Vey"* CD, from SillyMusic.com is the touching story of the six-pointed star-crossed lovers, Samuel Baum and Mae Feinberg, who find romance at the bridge table, to the horror and consternation of their grown children who oppose the match.

"Goys and Dolls," another CD from <u>SillyMusic.com</u>, tells the story of Jerome Schwartzberg, a nice Jewish boy who strays, thinking he'd be happier as a *"goy"* (gentile), dating a *"shiksa"* (gentile woman). With the help of his loving, if slightly overbearing family and a hyperactive *"shadchen"* (matchmaker), he finds his way back to the fold.

———◆———

The *YIVO* standard orthography is the most widely accepted method of spelling *Yiddish* words.

———◆———

There is a *YIVO* in Argentina; they spell it *IWO*. It is not exactly a branch, but more of an independent franchise.

———◆———

"Keshi-Meshi" was an old *Yiddish* radio jingle.

Do you itch? Buy Keshi-Meshi. Keshi-Meshi is the best cockroach powder in the whole world. It's very easy to apply the Keshi-Meshi: take the cockroach in one hand; take the Keshi-Meshi in the other hand. Pour out a little Keshi-Meshi on the cockroach — it should kill him very well. And if the Keshi-Meshi doesn't kill the cockroach, take the cockroach, place it in an envelope, and send him to us, the Keshi-Meshi company, and we'll make an end of him.

And in *Yiddish*,

S'Kratzt zikh? Koyft Keshi-Meshi. Keshi-Meshi iz di beste cockroach powder in gantzon velt. S'iz zeyr poshut tzu benutzn dem Keshi-Meshi: nemt dem cockroach in eyn hand; nemt dem Keshi-Meshi in anderen hand. Shit arayn a bisl Keshi-Meshi afn cockroach — es vet im gantz gut hargenen. Un az der Keshi-Meshi harget dem cockroach nit, nem dem cockroach, shtelt im in an anvelop, un shikt im tzu undz, di Keshi-Meshi kompani, un mir veln makhn a soyf fum im.

Reprinted from the e-mail list
Mendele: <u>Yiddish Literature and Language</u>,
Vol. 4.398

Sholem Aleichem died in the Bronx in 1916, and was laid to rest among "the common folk" in the Workmen's Circle Section of Mt. Carmel Cemetery in Brooklyn. His humble epitaph, which he had written for himself several years before his death, read as follows:

Do ligt a yid a posheter
Geshriben Yidish-Taytsh far vayber
Un far'n prosten folk hot er
Geven a humorist, a shrayber

Dos gantse lebn oysgelakht
Geshlogn mit der velt kapores
De gantse velt hot gut gemakht
Un er — oy vey — geven af tsoris.

Un davke demolt ven der oylem hot
Gelakht, geklatsht un fleg, zikh freyen
Hot er gekrenkt — dos veyst nor Got
B'sod, az keyner zol nit zeyn.

Here lies a simple Jew
Who wrote *Yiddish* tales for women
And for the common folk
He was a humorist, a writer.

His whole life he laughed
And joined the world in its reveries
The whole world enjoyed itself
While he — oy vey — had troubles.

And even as the public
Laughed, split their sides, whooped it up
He grieved, as only God knows
In secret, so that no one should see.

Used with permission
Pakn Treger,
The National Book Center

The Daily Forward once featured a section called "Gallery of Missing Husbands." It featured photos of men who ran away from their wives and families to begin anew with someone else. "*Galerye fun farshvundene mener*" is the official title of that section of the paper.

"*Luftmensch*," according to the 2004 Page A Day Calendar, is a quirky word.

The first reported use of the word "*chutzpah*" (in a state judicial opinion) was in Williams v. State (1972), an opinion of the Georgia Court of Appeals addressing an individual who broke into a sheriff's office to steal guns. The decision in Williams was written by Judge Clark who went on to write opinions using the *Yiddish* words "*schmooze,*" "*tsoriss,*" "*shammes,*" and "*gut gezacht.*" The word "*chutzpah*" was used in decisions by district courts in Iowa, Alabama, and Puerto Rico.

"*Shiksa lust*" reached its fullest expression in The Heartbreak Kid (1972). Charles Grodin leaves his Jewish bride (Jeannie Berlin) to pursue the golden girl of his dreams (Cybil Shepherd).

PHILOLOGOS (Forward: Arts & Letters) says that "Among New York Jews, in any case, the *Yiddish* word "*shpritz,*" literally a "splash" or a "squirt," is often referred to as plain seltzer. (The word "*seltzer*" itself comes from the German Selterser Wasser, named for the town of Selters in Germany, whose springs had a naturally bubbly water.)

"*Tsutcheppenish,*" according to Marty Fiebert, is defined as something irritating that attaches itself like an obsession.

Ex.: "She has a *tsutcheppenish* that is driving everyone crazy."

If you type the name "*Chaim*" into Microsoft SpellCheck, it comes up wrong.

David Friedman, JTA's former Washington bureau chief, died in 2003. Friedman often tried to put pun headlines on stories. When an Israeli politician whose last name was Gur lost an election, Friedman headlined the piece, "*Gur nicht!*" "*Gur nothing,*" drawing on *Yiddish* humor.

THE MENSCH

There once were two evil brothers. They were rich and used their money to keep their evil ways from the public eye. They attended the same temple, and to everyone else, they appeared to be perfect Jews.

One day, their rabbi retired and a new one was hired. Not only could the new rabbi see right through the brothers' deceptions, but he also spoke well and true about it. Due to the rabbi's honesty and integrity, the temple's membership grew in numbers. Eventually, a fundraising campaign was started to build a much bigger temple.

All of a sudden, one of the brothers died. The remaining brother sought out the new rabbi the day before the funeral and handed him a check for the amount needed to complete the new building. He held the check for the rabbi to see. 'I have only one condition," he said. "At the funeral, you must say my brother was a *mensch*. You must say those exact words."

After some thought, the rabbi gave his word and took the check. He cashed it immediately.

At the funeral the next day, however, the rabbi did not hold back. "He was an evil man," he said about the dead brother. "He cheated on his wife and abused his family. Never once did he commit an unselfish act." He railed on and on about the deceased. After nearly a half hour of the evil truth, the rabbi paused and shrugged his shoulders. Finally, he said, "But compared to his brother, he was a *mensch*."

— Source unknown

———————◆———————

The Russian writer, Maxim Gorky, acted as a *"Shabbos Goy"* in his youth.

———————◆———————

Sid Caesar's father, Max, was a *"Shabbos Goy"*; for a penny he would turn on lights and stoves for more observant Jews who would not perform such activities on the Sabbath.

———————◆———————

Beginning the summer of 2004, anyone can log onto the website of the *National Yiddish Book Center* (www.yiddishbookcenter.org) and read the complete text of any *Yiddish* book in their collection, FREE of charge.

This homiletic tale is titled, "The Rabbi's Sermon":

> In a large Florida city, the local rabbi developed quite a reputation for his sermons; so much so that everyone in the community came every Shabbos.
>
> Unfortunately, one weekend a member had to visit Long Island for his nephew's Bar Mitzvah. But he didn't want to miss The Rabbi's sermon. So he decided to hire a *"Shabbos goy"* to sit in the congregation and tape the sermon so he could listen to it when he returned.
>
> Other congregants saw what was going on, and they also decided to hire *"Shabbos goyim"* to tape the sermon so they could play golf instead of going to shul. Within a few weeks time there were 500 gentiles sitting in *shul* taping the Rabbi.
>
> The Rabbi got wise to this. The following Shabbos he, too, hired a *Shabbos goy* who brought a tape recorder to play his prerecorded sermon to the 500 gentiles in the congregation who dutifully recorded his words on their machines.
>
> Witnesses said this marked the first incidence in history of "artificial *insermonation.*"

"Pripetshik" is a *Yiddish* immersion program for children who are being raised with *Yiddish*.

The song, *"Oyfn Pripetshik"* means "On the Hearth." It was used in Steven Spielberg's "Schindler's List."

In *Yiddish*, *"knipl"* means a housewife's nest egg.

Letty Cottin Pogrebin ("Deborah, Golda, & Me") wrote that her mother had a *"Knippel"* — a secret purse. Ms. Pogrebin said that "Her *knippel* taught me early on that money is freedom and a woman should always have something of her own, just in case."

"Julius *Knipl*" was the title character of Ben Katchor's weekly comic strip.

Mark Evanier (www.POVonline.com) wrote of the machinations of Bialystock and Bloom in the Broadway show, The Producers: "Instead of not caring if there is failure, they actively covet it. Other than that, the modus operandi is the same: The guys who set up the pyramid flee to Rio with the bucks while the investors get *bupkis*."

———◆———

A *"teppel"* is the *Yiddish* word for bowl or ladle.

———◆———

Sid Caesar wrote about how humor was an outgrowth of the misunderstandings between *Yiddish* and English. In his book, "Caesar's Hours — My life In Comedy, With Love And Laughter" he tells the story about an elderly woman who called over a waiter at one of the hotels in the Catskills. She told him, "Bring me a *bekked teppel*." So the waiter brought her one of those big ladles. She look at the ladle and yelled, "I wanted a *bekked teppel!*" "Oh, you wanted a baked apple!" the waiter "Why didn't you say so?"

———◆———

Sid Caesar played a Japanese character named *"Taka Mashuga"* (i.e. Really Crazy) on television.

———◆———

A *"boychik"* is *Yiddish* for boy — a term of endearment. In the 1974 movie, "The Apprenticeship of Duddy Kravitz," Joe Silver snapped five-spots at Richard Dreyfuss croacking, "Hey, *boychik!* Remember — I like snappy service!"

———◆———

"Yenta Telebente" is Mrs. National Enquirer, according to Zipple.com.

———◆———

Martin Bodek's quiz (Bang-itout.com) titled, "Who Wants to Marry a Boro Park Millionaire?" asked the following $2,000 question:

How do you say the word "cucumber" in *Yiddish*?

A) Kartofel   C) Igerkeh

B) Tzibileh   D) Gebeks

The correct answer is (C).

Sidney Lumet, the son of Baruch Lumet and Eugenia Wermus, veterans of the *Yiddish* stage, made his professional debut on radio at age four and his stage debut at the *Yiddish* Art Theatre at five. For two years during the Depression (1931-1932) he played the son in a *Yiddish* radio serial scripted and directed by his father called "The Rabbi From Brownsville."

In the 1962 movie, "A Majority of One," starring Rosalind Russell and Alec Guinness, Russell plays the part of Bertha Jacoby, a zaftig Jewish widow. Mrs. Jacoby keeps a kosher home and uses the following *Yiddish* terms: *gonif, meshugah, tsuris, kvelling*, and *schlemiel*. She also demanded that a rabbi be present when they filmed the final scene, in which she has to bless the sabbath candles. She herself was a devout Roman Catholic and wanted to make sure she got it right.

"Jewish *Shandes* (Scandals) That Shook The Modern World" was a 2004 course offering with Elderhostel. (The course investigates *shandes* committed by Meyer Lansky, Julius/Ethel Rosenberg, Michael Milkin, Amy Fisher, Heidi Fleiss, Chandra Levy and Monica Lewinsky and will be viewed in terms of its impact on the Jewish Community and the world at large.)

Ingrid Peritz (The Globe and Mail) wrote the following obituary for Dora Wasserman:

WEDNESDAY, DECEMBER 17, 2003

MONTREAL — If there were murmurs of *oy vey* on the streets of Montreal yesterday, the lament was understandable: Dora Wasserman, *maven* of Montreal theatre and champion of the *Yiddish* language, had passed away.

Ms. Wasserman's raw willpower helped keep alive a language whose death notice had been signed more than once. She believed *Yiddish* was all about survival, and it drove her to stage plays in the Displaced Persons Camps of Europe, and later to found the only resident *Yiddish* Theatre in North America . . .

In *Yiddish*, the plural of "finger" is "finger" — not fingers. And "finger" also means toe.

"Kenen oyf di finger" means to have (facts) at one's fingertips.

A *"grober finger"* is a thumb.

Aaron Lansky (<u>National Yiddish Book Center</u>) believes that "to rescue a culture, the first thing you do is rescue books."

Rabbi Steven Z. Leder (Wilshire Boulevard Temple, Los Angeles), defined "a *macher complex*" as someone who was addicted to being important.

According to Gil Student, a *"macher"* is a common *Yiddish* term. It seems that Rabbi Leder combined pop psychology with *Yiddish* to create a new hybrid term. I would take it at face value, keeping in mind that pop psychology is generally common sense with fancy terminology and not real science."

Ben Gailing, who launched the "<u>Yiddish Radio Show</u>" on WDLW — AM 1330, published a collection of sketches in his book, "<u>*Git a Shmeykhl.*</u>" The book contained titles like "He stitches *Matzos* on the Singer Machine," "An Interview with a Thanksgiving Turkey," and "The Busy Season in Heaven."

According to Jonathan Tobin (<u>Jewish World Review</u>),

> In his [1999] speech, Gore chose to go the all-out pander route to appeal to Jewish interests. The vice president used Hebrew and *Yiddish* words, and his mispronunciation of the word *chesed*; he pronounced the first two letters with a soft "ch," as in the word church — produced peals of knowing laughter from the audience.
>
> If that wasn't enough, the famously stiff veep read through a comedic list of "Jewish country and Western song titles." Though this was the sort of e-mail joke list that clutters most computers (i.e. "The second time she said '*shalom*' I knew she meant goodbye"), the goofy item was a 'big hit with listeners in Atlanta.

"*Mame — Loshn Kinder — Loshn*" is a documentary film by Avi Lehrer and Tommy Schwarcz. It reconstructs the history of *Yiddish* in Israel — from the boycott of the language by the new Israelis who wanted no connection to life in exile, to the present-day study of the language in universities and the staging of theater-filling *Yiddish*-language plays.

---◆---

The Workmen's Circle seder Hagode is rich with *Yiddish* songs about Peysakh happenings. In *Yiddish* translation, from the traditional Hagode was *Dayenu*:

Voltn mir nor fun Mitsrayim
Gliklekh oisgeleyzt gevorn
Nor der yam zikh nit geshpoltn - Dayienu

Volt der yam zikh shoyn geshpoltn
Nor im durkhgeyn in der trukh
Volt undz demolt nit gegoltn - Dayenu

Voltn mir im shoyn ariber
Nit gekent nor iberkumen
Fertsik yor in groysn midber - Dayenu

Voltn mir di fertsik yor shoyn
In dem midber durkgekumen
Un keyn man dort wit gefunen - Dayenu

Voltn mir dort man gefunen
Nor dem shabes nit bakumen
Un tsum Sinay nit gekumen - Dayenu

Voltn mir tsum Sinay kumen
Nor di toyre nit bakumen
S'folk fun toyre nit gevorn - Dayenu.

---◆---

Michael Feldman ("<u>Whad' Ya Know?</u>") wrote about don'ts:

"don't be afraid to ring the meat butcher" ("they keep the good chickens in back");

"don't start with the neighbors', ("a *shonda hopa mit* the neighbors,') . . .

The second sentence could be labeled "corrupted Yinglish" — not *Yiddish*. "A *shande un a kharpe far di skheynim*" means a shame and a scandal for the neighbors.

A "*baleboosteh*," according to Michael D. Fein (The Gantseh Megillah), is the mistress of the house. A compliment to someone who is a terrific housekeeper. "She is some *baleboosteh*!"

Bubba's *Yiddish* Glossary (bubbygram.com) defines a "*beryiah*" as a *baleboosteh* squared; a regular Martha Stewart. A homemaker who puts the rest of us to shame.

Philip Roth's definition of a "*ballabuste*":

"She practically sleeps with a dustcloth in her hand."

The AISH Rabbi says "that a "*balabustah* is one of those jerry-rigged linguistic anomalies — two Hebrew words welded together with a *Yiddish* suffix. '*Bal*' means boss, '*bayis*' means house, and '*tah*' is an endearing suffix. *Balabustah* connotes a woman in charge of her domain."

Yungtruf ("Call to Youth"), a worldwide organization of *Yiddish*-speaking and *Yiddish*-learning adults, was founded in 1964 to give the younger generation an opportunity to get together to speak *Yiddish*, to read and study *Yiddish* literature, and to write, sing and socialize in *Yiddish*.

"*Plotz*," according to The Alternative *Yiddish* Dictionary, is defined as follows:

> (verb) Fall down dead right now. "Ham and cheese sandwiches? If your grandfather weren't already dead, he'd *plotz*."

In *Yiddish*, a female gentile can be "*goye*" or "*goyke*."

The New Yorker Magazine ("The Back Page by Pete Hamill") once offered the NYAT (New York Aptitude Test). Question No. 20 was, "What is the difference between a '*schlemiel*' and a '*schlimazel*'?" His answer: A *schlemiel* is unlucky, whereas a *schlimazel* is simply inept.

According to Bubba's *Yiddish* Glossary, a "*machashafeh*" is a witch, a conjurer, someone with psychic or supernatural powers.

"*Ferfoilt*" is spoilt, mildewed, rotten, decayed. Ex. "Marvin, you're 36 years old already. Time to get rid of that *ferfoilteh shmata!*" (rotten rag, or in this instance, lousy security blanket.)

A "*boorivka*," according to Bubba's *Yiddish* Glossary, is literally, a blueberry. Colloquially used, it refers to a large dark mole. "That Robert Redford is so handsome, but *oi!* all those *boorivkas!*"

Rabbi Emanuel S. Goldsmith recorded, "I Really Love Yiddish: A Mini-Course in Yiddish Based on Literature, Folklore and Humor." Goldsmith said, "I believe with perfect faith that there will be a revival of interest in *Yiddish*."

Sylvia Schildt is the author of "*Mayn Shtetele Bronzvil*." The following paragraphs were preliminary writings that led up to the book:

I can recall countless Saturday nights during my seventeen summers at 38 Herzl Street (around the corner from Pitkin Avenue) and there are four extremely pleasant things I remember most. The first is sitting with the grown-ups in front of the entrance to our apartment building (on a wooden milk box, cushioned with old newspapers) and tuning into their talk — it was sometimes in *Yiddish*, sometimes in Brooklynese, and sometimes in a mishmash of both, with a little Russian or Polish tossed in. It was war talk, political talk, personal gossip, complaints about shortages and rationing, plus therapy sessions and arguments about "*di kinder*" followed by a lot of sighing.

I remember the beckoning lights of Pitkin Avenue and the comings and goings. Inflation is burning was a running thread in conversations. I remember being sent to the newsstand on Strauss Street for the _Forverts_, The Tog, The Morgn Zhurnal, The Freyhayt, The Post, News, Mirror, Daily Worker, even the Times.

———◆———

In 1936, *Yiddish* playwright, actor, and linguist, Nahum Stutchkoff premiered his great radio drama, *Bei Tate-mames Tish* (Round the Family Table), sponsored by Manischewitz Matzo. And in 1937, he staged *Der Land fun Khaloymes* (The Land of Dreams).

In 1946, Stutchkoff debuted a new radio drama called *Tsures ba Leitn* (People's Problems), sponsored by the Brooklyn Jewish Chronic Disease Hospital.

———◆———

The *Yiddish* word for hipsters, according to Steven I. Weiss and Zackary Sholem Berger, is "*artist'n*."

———◆———

"*Nakhes*" (also spelled "*naches*" and "*nachas*") means pleasure, mixed with pride. Rabbi Harold M. Schulweis once quipped that we Jews need to measure things in terms of the GNP — the Gross *Nachas*-Producing amount.

103

Rabbi Norm Shifren (AKA "the Surfing Rabbi") has been riding the Malibu surf for more than 40 years and is founder of Jewish Surfers International. Rabbi Shifrin offers the following surfing terms in *Yiddish*:

> *Verplatzed* — When one is stunned by a wipe out and doesn't know to swim up or down.
>
> *Farblunged* — When a person doesn't even know where the beach is.
>
> *Farmished* — Taking the wrong freeway offramp to get to the beach.
>
> *Treifed Out* — After surfing several hours and building up a mighty appetite, only to find that the restaurant has no kosher food.
>
> *Shaloha* — A greeting to a Jewish surfer.

———◆———

Clyde Haberman, columnist for <u>The New York Times</u>, wrote a piece on Jan. 6, 2004 titled, "A City Full Of Material For Reality TV." He said, "A city as diverse as New York provides no shortage of potential programs based on stereotypes long recognized as crude. . . In '*Yiddishe* Brains for the Goyishe Guy,' five Jewish financial advisers provide a gentile man with investment tips."

———◆———

Theodore Bikel has played the Tevye role more than 2,000 times since 1967. Bikel fashioned his Tevye after his own "*zeydeh*," Reb Shimon Bikel.

———◆———

Brooklyn (NY) Borough President, Marty Markowitz, asked the City Transportation Department for a sign on the Williamsburg Bridge reading "Leaving Brooklyn: *Oy Vey!*" The agency said the sign — featuring the *Yiddish* phrase for "*oh, woe*" — would be too distracting for motorists. (The city earlier nixed a sign reading "Leaving Brooklyn: Fuhgeddaboudit!" at the Verazzano Narrows Bridge for the same reason.)

———◆———

"*Der Zeyde*" or "*zeydeh*" is the grandfather.
"*Di Zeyde-bobe*" are the grandparents.

One of the best modern *Yiddish* poets/songwriters is Beyle Schaechter-Gottesman. One of her recent *Yiddish* children's song collection is titled,

Fli, mayn flishlang
(Fly, my kite)

Original *Yiddish* Children's Songs
by Beyle Schaechter-Gottesman
©1999 Boyle Schaechter-Gottesman
New York

I thank her for permission to reprint it.

FLI, MAYN FLISHLANG
Vos flit es dortn oybn?
An eroplan, tsi a foygl?
Nisht keyn eroplan, nisht keyn foygl,
Mayn flishlang flit dortn oybn!
Fli, mayn flishlang, fli,
In di heykhn tsi,
Iber khmares un roykh,
Hoykh, hoykh, hoykh!

Fli, mayn flishlang, vayt,
Biz af yener zayt.
Vu s'hot di velt an ek,
Avek, avek, avek!
Tra-la-la-la-la (2)
Vu s'hut di velt an ek,
Avek, avek, avek!

Vos flit es dortn oybn?
Nisht keyn eroplan,
Nisht keyn foygl,
Siz nisht keyn — neyn, nisht keyn flig.
Mayn flishlang kumt tsurik.
Tra-la-la-la-la (2)
S'iz nisht keyn — neyn, nisht keyn flig.
Mayn flishlang kumt tsurik.

Is it an airplane or a bird up there? No, it's my kite above the clouds and smoke.

Fly, my kite, fly to the end of the world.

"Zingen" means to sing. *"Zingen ken ikh nit, ober a mayvn bin ikh"* means, "I can't sing a note, but I know all about it." *"Es iz gut tsu zingen un tantsen"* means, "It's good to sing and dance."

"Der nign" (or niggun) is a melody without words, a melody sung using "ya-dai-dai," "bim-bom," or some other equally universal sounds, rather than words.

Rabbi Stephen Pearce (senior rabbi at the Reform Congregation Emanu-El in San Francisco) wrote,

> Sholom Secunda, a Russian-born songwriter, composed the *Yiddish* song. "*Bei mir bist du schon*" (To Me You Are Beautiful) in 1932. Secunda begged the then-megastar Eddie Cantor to introduce his hit song on his radio show. Cantor declined, saying, "Sholom, I love your music. But I can't use it. It's too Jewish."

> Sammy Cahn, another Jewish songwriter, convinced the popular Andrews Sisters to record the lyrics of Secunda's song that he translated from the *Yiddish* into an English rendition. The song's sales took off with the purchase of a quarter of a million records and 200,000 copies of sheet music in a one-month period.

Professor Eliezer L. Segal ("<u>Why Didn't I Learn This in Hebrew School?</u>") told the following charming anecdote about Rabbah Gamaliel, who blessed his daughter on the birth of her first child with the rather upsetting prayer "May the word '*vay*' never budge from your lips." When his daughter voiced her dismay at receiving such a "blessing," the doting *zeydeh* explained his real intention. His wish was that she might have many occasions to lament about such domestic "troubles" as "*Vay*, my baby won't eat! *Vay*, my baby doesn't want to go to school!" Rabbah Gamaliel astutely perceived that there are certain types of parental torments that we learn to prefer over the alternatives.

And just so that you should not be mistaken into supposing that Jews only knew how to suffer, we should make it clear that talmudic literature knows also of an appropriate interjection for joyous occasions: "Wah!" The similarity between the sounds of way and wah often furnished occasions for elaborate word-plays, which hinted subtly at just how fragile the borderline between sorrow and joy often is.

(The original source: Genesis Rabbah 26:4)

◆

"*Yiddish* is special in that its speakers continue to be bilingual or multilingual, thus triggering continuous borrowing," says Professor Ellen Prince. Prince collected classified ads ("*Klasifayd* Eds") from the <u>Forverts</u>, written by the "man in the street" without concern for what is "right" or "elegant." The borrowings are in caps.

> PEYNTER — ineveynik, oysnveyni, PLASTERING, fraye ESTMEYTS. RUM $45, fentster $5. george painting cont. 932-1412 (3/22/85; p. 41)

> BIZNESMAN zukht FOYNISHD RUM. manhetn oder kvins. best REFERENSES. call after 6 p.m. wa8-4863 (3/22/85)

> ratner's DEYRI restoran. barimt far di veste heymishe gebeksn. mir KEYTERN oykh tsu alerley simkhes un andere. private BOLRUMS. plats far 80 biz 800 mentshn. (2/6/87; p. 26)

> groys FOYRNISHD RUM mit KITSHEN, LIVING RUM, PORTSH privilegies, YUTILITIS (718-5169.) (3/22/85; p. 41)

◆

Lillian Lux hosted a weekly radio program on WEVD called "<u>Yiddish Stars of Yesterday</u>."

According to the Straight Dope Science Advisory Board, "If you don't like baseball, you would say "baseball *schmaseball*."

———◆———

Jenna Weissman Joselit wrote in a <u>Forward</u> newspaper column titled, "The Wonders of America" (July 12, 2002),

> While baseball, too, had wore than its fair share of *Yiddish*-speaking fans, quite a number of immigrant Jews found its language, gestures, and sensibility baffling, if not utterly incomprehensible . . . immigrant Jews mistake "*pisher*" for "*pitcher*"; in another, they're convinced that "Lynch the Umpire" is the man's name, not a call to action and, in still another scenario, a first-time visitor to a baseball stadium, seeing hordes of people on their feet, screaming and yelling, can only conclude that a union rally is under way.

———◆———

Yiddish humorist, Louis Markowitz, wrote a monologue called "*Berl Bass Shpilt Beysbol*" in the 1930s, which was performed by poet/actor Zvee Scooler ("Der Grammeister") on New York station WEVD. It was also parlayed to great success by *Yiddish* comic Michi Rosenberg, in performance (and on Banner Records) as "Getsl at a Baseball Game."

———◆———

The song "<u>Take Me Out to the Ballgame</u>" was written by Jack Norworth and Albert Von Tilzer. The *Yiddish* lyrics were written by Henry Sapoznik and are included here with his permission.

Fir mir oys tsu der bolgeym.
Tsum oylem lomir dokh geyn
Keyf mir di nisleh un kreker jek
Vil ikh keynmol fin dort geyn avek
Vayl men shrayt "Vivat!" far di shpiler
s'iz a shande az men farshpilt
Vayl s'iz "eyns, tsvey, dray" strikes bist "oys!"
In der beysbol geym.

"Saichel" or *"seikhhel"* means common sense. The late Marlene Adler Marks wrote an article for <u>Jewish World Review</u> in which she said, "Frieda Loehmann's Bronx discount center, which started in 1920 with the goods procured from her garment-center friends, once symbolized a certain wildly prized kind of shopping *seikhel* that must be counted among Jewry's gifts to America. Long before Donald Trump wrote <u>"The Art of the Deal</u>," we were practicing it here, in Loehmann's Back Room, where designer labels were obliterated but not quite cutoff, indicating to the discerning buyer that standards were being maintained."

———————◆———————

A *"Yeshivish car"* is a car driven by someone who attends *Yeshiva* and typically drives a jalopy as nobody expects anybody from a *Yeshiva* to be able to afford better.

———————◆———————

Tovah Feldshuh starred as Golda Meir in the Broadway show, <u>Golda's Balcony</u>. In a vigorous portrayal of the prime minister, she relates how Goldele was greeted by 50,000 Jews outside of a Moscow synagogue. She was so shaken that she couldn't think of anything to say except, *"A dank eich vos ihr seit geblieben Yidden."* (Thank you for remaining Jews.)

———————◆———————

"Tsuriktsien zikh" means retire, to (stop working). Actor-writer-director and very funny man Mel Brooks, talks about working and retirement: "Do I lift, do I drive, am I bagging groceries at a very busy supermarket? No, I sit with a little pencil and if I have an idea, I write it down. It's light work. I can do that forever."

———————◆———————

The last five words of the play, <u>"Golda's Balcony</u>," by William Gibson are:

Shalom. Shalom. Shalom. Shalom. Shalom. . .

GLOSSARY

Abi Gezunt	As long as you're healthy
Balabuste	Excellent and praiseworthy homemaker
Bashert	Predestined; inevitable
Bialy	Round bread roll, topped with flakes of onion
Bissel	Little bit
Bobkes	Nothing
Bubbeh mayseh	Grandmother's story; an unbelievable tale
Bubelah	Diminitive term of endearment for a child
Chai	Number 18; root of the expression, "L'Chaim"
Chozzerai	Junk
Chuppah	Bridal canopy
Chutzpah	Nerve
Dreck	Manure
Farbissina	Dour; mean; unpleasant; a word so good it made it into the Austin Powers films
Fraylech	Happy
Gantseh k'nocker	Big shot!
Gantseh megillah	Big deal! (derisive); a popular Yiddish website
Gelt	Money
Gonif	Thief
Gottenyu	Oh God! (anguished cry)
Goy	Gentile; non-observant Jew
Kibbitzer	Meddlesome spectator
Kineahora	Knock on wood
Klutz	Ungraceful; awkward
Kvell	To get pleasure from
Kvetch	Complain
Luftmensch	Person with no business, trade, calling or income; builds castles in the air
Macher	Man with contacts
Maven	Expert
Mecheich	Something delicious. Ex. Jackie Mason's Famous Broadway Cheesecake, produced by Rhoda's Best
Mensch	Special man or person

GLOSSARY

Mitzvah	Good deed
Nishdugedacht	It shouldn't happen! God forbid!
Ongepotchket	Overdone; thrown together without planning
Oy!!	Exclamation to denote pain, disgust, astonishment or rapture
Putz	Curse word, referring to penis; a stupid person
Schmendrick	Nincompoop; fool
Schmutz	Dirt; slime
Shande	Shame
Shadchen	Matchmaker
Shikseh	Non-Jewish girl
Shlep	Drag or pull
Shpilkes	To be uneasy; stressed out
Shtik	Rap, routine or an m.o. Jack Benny's shtik was being 39 and cheap
Shtuppa	Vulgarism for sexual intercourse
Shul	Synagogue
Shvitz	Perspire
Tate	Father
Trayf	Forbidden food; impure
Tsuris	Troubles; misery
Vunderlich	Wonderful
Yenta	Female who is involved in everyone's business; a gossipy woman
Yid	Jew (male or female)
Yiddisher Kop	Jewish head

Note: There are many different spellings for *Yiddish* words.